Adolescent Parenthood and Education
Exploring Alternative Programs

Mary Pilat

D1457666

T5 - BYX - 438

GARLAND PUBLISHING, INC.
New York & London
1997

Library of Congress Cataloging-in-Publication Data

Pilat, Mary.
    Adolescent parenthood and education : exploring alternative
programs / by Mary Pilat.
        p.   cm. — (Michigan State University series on children,
youth, and families ; v. 2) (Garland reference library of social
science ; v. 1004)
    Includes bibliographical references and index.
    ISBN 0-8153-1884-7 (alk. paper)
    1. Pregnant schoolgirls—Education—United States.   2. Teenage
mothers—Education—United States.   3. Alternative education—
United States.   I. Title.   II. Series.   III. Series: Garland reference
library of social science ; v. 1004.
LC4091.P496   1997
371.96'7—dc20   96-35890
                                              CIP

Printed on acid-free, 250-year-life paper
Manufactured in the United States of America

For Veronica, Lee-Anne, and Sara

Service delivery to pregnant and parenting teens is a complex system of individual and organizational stakeholders in a dynamic setting.

Adolescent parenting is not a problem to be solved but a reality to be lived.

Contents

List of Figures and Tables

Series Editor's Preface

The publication of Mary Pilat's volume, *Adolescent Parenthood and Education: Exploring Alternative Programs*, signals the continued successful development of the Michigan State University Series on Children, Youth, and Families. Pilat's scholarly work exemplifies the intent of the books in the MSU Series—a focus on issues of social policy, program design and delivery, and evaluation that address the needs of a diversity of children, youth, families, and communities.

Mary Pilat's volume is also a clear illustration of the goals of the Institute for Children, Youth, and Families (ICYF), which initiated the series, in particular as an example of the relationship of outreach scholarship to policy issues and intervention design. The mission of the Institute for Children, Youth, and Families at MSU is based on a vision of the nature of a land-grant institution as an academic unit with a responsibility for addressing the welfare of children, youth, and families in communities. More specifically, the mission of ICYF is shaped by an ecological perspective to human development that places the life span development of human beings in the context of the significant settings of human experience, including community, family, work and peer networks (Lerner, et al., 1994; Schiamberg, 1985, 1988). Historically, the ecological perspective has been both associated with, and a guiding frame for, colleges of home economics or, as they are more recently termed, colleges of human ecology, human development, or family and consumer sciences (Miller & Lerner, 1994).

Using the ecology of human development perspective as a conceptual framework, ICYF continues to develop programs that integrate the critical notion of development in context with the attempt, indeed the necessity, of creating connections between such scholarship and social policy, program design, delivery, and evaluation.

The MSU Series, under the committed and scholarly leadership of Senior Editor John Paul McKinney and the able guidance of Marie Ellen Larcada of Garland Publishing, provides a vehicle for the communication of collaborative research and outreach efforts. The series publishes reference and professional books, including monographs and edited volumes, that appeal to a wide audience in communities and universities, including such constituent groups as scholars, practitioners, service deliverers, child and family advocates, business leaders, and policymakers.

The unique role and perspective of both ICYF and the MSU Series can be further appreciated in light of ongoing and persisting trends for both university accountability and social contribution. In particular, the various university stakeholders, including business, government, and community leadership, are increasingly urging universities to use their research and scholarly resources to address problems of social, political, and technological relevance (Boyer, 1990; Votruba, 1992). Thus, communities are seeking a greater involvement in outreach on the part of their universities. The Institute for Children, Youth, and Families and Michigan State University are both committed to integrating outreach into the full fabric of university responsibility (Provost's Committee on University Outreach, 1993; Lerner and Simon, in press).

Mary Pilat's work is a valuable contribution to this emerging outreach/research focus. *Adolescent Parenthood and Education* represents the careful thinking of an author who has worked, first hand, with community programs that reflect both success and "best practice" in the field of adolescent parenting. There is a compelling need for intervention programs that reflect such careful thinking and best practice in addressing the circumstances of adolescent mothers who face not only the developmental issues of their offspring but the challenges of their own adolescence as well.

The MSU Series editors as well as the staff of the Institute for Children, Youth, and Families at MSU are grateful to have this volume on the critical social issue of adolescent pregnancy as part of the MSU Series.

Lawrence B. Schiamberg

References

Boyer, E. L. (1990). *Scholarship reconsidered: Priorities of the professoriate.* Princeton, NJ: The Carnegie Foundation for the Advancement of Teaching.

Boyer, E. L. (1994, March 9). Creating the new American college [Point of View column]. *The Chronicle of Higher Education* (p. A48).

Lerner, R. M., & Miller, J. R. (1993). Integrating human development research and intervention for America's children: The Michigan State University model. *Journal of Applied Developmental Psychology, 14,* 347–364.

Lerner, R. M., Miller, J. R., Knott, J. H., Corey, K. E., Bynum, T. S., Hoopfer, L. C., McKinney, M. H., Abrams, L. A., Hula, R. C., & Terry, P. A. (1994). Integrating scholarship and outreach in human development research, policy, and service: A developmental contextual perspective. In D. L. Featherman, R. M. Lerner, & M. Perlmutter (Eds.), *Life-span development and behavior, 12* (pp. 249–273). Hillsdale, NJ: Erlbaum.

Lerner, R. M. & Simon, L. A. K. (eds.)(in press). *Creating the new outreach university for America's youth and families: Building university-community collaborations for the twenty-first century.* New York: Garland.

Lerner, R. M., Terry, P. A., McKinney, M. H., & Abrams, L. A. (1994). Addressing child poverty within the context of a community-collaborative university: Comments on Fabes, Martin, and Smith (1994) and McLoyd (1994). *Family and Consumer Sciences Research Journal, 23,* 67–75.

Miller, J. R., & Lerner, R. M. (1994). Integrating research and outreach: Developmental contextualism and the human ecological perspective. *Home Economics Forum, 7,* 21–28.

Provost's Committee on University Outreach (1993). *University outreach at Michigan State University: Extending knowledge to serve society.* A report by the Provost's Committee on University Outreach. Michigan State University. East Lansing: Michigan State University.

Votruba, J. C. (1992). Promoting the extension of knowledge in service to society. *Metropolitan Universities, 3* (3), 72–80.

Foreword

Adolescent pregnancy and parenting continue to be topics of intense debate in our country. We find it difficult to be neutral or disinterested regarding issues surrounding the birth and rearing of children, particularly when the parents in question are the very young. Opinions run the gamut, and often polarizations occur. As a nation, we have not come to any agreement regarding the underlying questions and appropriate solutions. All too often, opinions are formed and assumptions are made based on inadequate, incomplete, or even biased information. Mary Pilat's *Adolescent Parenthood and Education: Exploring Alternative Programs* contributes to our understanding of early childbearing and the community's response by presenting information that is both scientific and sensitive. Practitioners, policy makers, and concerned citizens will benefit from the author's insights on educational programs for young parents.

To both appreciate the need for Pilat's book and to better frame the issues of teenage pregnancy, it is helpful to raise several essential questions. First, *who are the teenagers in question and why are they worthy of our attention?* Second, *what is an adequate, ethical response?* In answer to the first question, recent data on teenage sexuality, teen pregnancy, and teen birth rates provide us with many of the necessary insights. In our country, 50 percent of all females and 75 percent of all males are sexually active by age 18. At the time of first intercourse, 96 percent of teenage women are unmarried. Interestingly, the rates of sexual activity among America's teenagers are quite similar to those of other Western industrialized nations. However, when it comes to rates of *pregnancy, birth, and abortions* among teens, the United States has significantly higher rates than any other industrialized country. This is not news. It has been that way for some time now. These statistics are difficult for Americans to acknowledge and understand.

Research over the last two decades has shed light on the factors that contribute to the higher rates of childbearing among our nation's young. It is not surprising that issues confronting our society as a whole affect our young people. That is, early pregnancy has been linked to the economic climate, family stress, physical and sexual abuse, substance abuse, school performance, self-esteem, and other social and psychological factors. Specifically, teenagers who have been raised in single-parent homes, are poor, have low academic achievement, have matured early, or have had early *involuntary* sex are at highest risk. Many families lack the economic, social, and emotional resources they need to raise their children in a healthy environment. Since there is no single cause, it is important that early pregnancy in the United States be understood within the larger social context in which it occurs.

Because of the multiplicity of causal factors of teenage pregnancy, prevention has been difficult. Furthermore, it is clear that no single intervention will prevent teen pregnancy. Effective prevention requires interventions that realistically address the diverse and multiple needs of the American teenager. Although recent statistics indicate that the number of births to teens declined somewhat in 1992 and 1993, it should be noted that this decline was concentrated among older teenagers, with births to teenagers under 17 rising slightly during that period. In addition, while the rate of actual births is declining, the number of teenage women in our country is increasing substantially. Between 1995 and 2005, the population of teen women between 14 and 17 is expected to increase by some 1.2 million. What does this mean in actual numbers? In 1993, there were 513,647 births to women under the age of 20. Even if the birth rate remains stable or goes down, the actual numbers of births to teenage women can be expected to increase over the next ten years. These numbers are more than sufficient to warrant our attention.

While we have not yet been successful in significantly reducing pregnancies and births among our teenagers, we have learned a great deal about providing effective interventions once pregnancy has occurred. Teenage pregnancy and parenthood are associated with very serious social, emotional, physical, psychological, and economic challenges, not only to the young parents and their children, but to the larger society as well. Working with pregnant and parenting teenagers is a form of *secondary* prevention, reducing the risks and ensuring healthy outcomes.

Young parents are often ill-equipped to meet the challenges they face. Since they are still adolescents themselves, they are faced with the dual responsibilities of meeting their own developmental needs and those of their children. Their resources are limited, and, without high school diplomas, they are unlikely to find jobs that can meet their financial responsibilities. Quality day-care for infants is difficult to find, and when available, the cost often far exceeds the economic resources available. School dropout frequently results. Further, most teenagers are inadequately trained in parenting skills. Paternal involvement in parenting and financial responsibility is often lacking. When the fathers of the children are involved, the couple relationships are challenging. Relationships with peers, a key factor in the life of developing teenagers, are forever altered. As a result, many teen parents find themselves isolated, cut off from services and support systems.

In the face of these monumental challenges, it is no surprise that the children of teenage parents are at higher risk for complications, such as low birth weight and birth defects. Furthermore, there is some evidence that these children are more likely to die during their first year and during childhood have more health problems and compromised educational achievement and socioemotional adaptation.

In terms of what constitutes both an adequate and an ethical response to these conditions, it is clear that, as a society, we have a continuing responsibility to address both prevention and intervention. Without appropriate support services, many teen parents may face a downhill spiral of school dropout, welfare dependency, continued unplanned pregnancies, and long-term negative consequences for themselves and their children. Over the course of the last twenty-five years, programs have been developed to respond to the unique and multiple needs of pregnant and parenting teens. In order to adequately address the complex challenges and ameliorate the negative consequences, these programs must be comprehensive in nature, providing access to a broad range of services.

We now know that attendance in a comprehensive program can have positive outcomes in terms of secondary prevention, reducing the rates of school dropout, unintended repeat pregnancies, complications of pregnancy, and birth defects. We also know that completion of high school and the development of job skills make welfare dependency much less likely. Assistance with options and parenting classes make it possible for teenagers to develop and carry out successful plans for rearing their children. Six areas have been identified as key to ensuring successful outcomes for childbearing teenagers and their children: health care, education, counseling, child care, social services, and job training. To develop an adequate response, a community must call forth the varied expertise of health care providers, social workers, counselors, educators, and other support persons.

In her landmark study, Mary Pilat has taken the field of service provision to a higher level, exploring not only what works but why. While statistics on outcomes of a diversity of teen parent programs have been collected, her study is unique in addressing what is required to make a program work, not only from the viewpoint of the service provider, but from the perspectives of all of the stakeholders: young parents, support persons, staff, administrators, and policy makers. Drawing on her personal experience as coordinator of a cooperative education program for childbearing teenagers, she is in a particularly good position to address the issues and concerns of all participants in the complex system of teenage pregnancy and parenting. In fact, it was her need to address matters of practice and policy that prompted her to move from a focused career in service provision to a broader pursuit of the research that is the basis for this book. Thus, she provides the reader not only with workable program models, but also with the experiential insight necessary to identify strategies that work. Pilat takes both a focused view, revealing the intricacies of what is required to put successful programs together, as well as a broader perspective, identifying the unique challenges of developing and maintaining these programs in national, state, county, and local contexts and circumstances. She has managed to capture not only the complicated nature of service provision, but the emotional and psychological complexities as well, transmitted through the voices that matter most—the people who are themselves involved.

Of particular interest are the viewpoints of the stakeholders—teenagers and service providers alike. In Chapter 5, we hear from the adolescent parents themselves. Through the voice of Jamie, we come to understand the ongoing hardships and challenges faced by a young mother raising her son. She explains why attendance in an alternative school has been significant, offering her opportunities to complete her education, learn to be a good parent, and face the complexities of her life. Often overlooked is the crucial role played by significant others in the teen parent's life. In Chapter 6, we hear those "voices of support" and learn about their own needs to be supported as well. Jamie's story, along with those of the other teen parents and care providers interviewed by the author, represents a key contribution of the author to the literature on teen pregnancy and parenthood—the experiential verification of the issues of teen pregnancy in the words of the teen mothers and providers themselves.

Because of my own experiences as a teacher and counselor in a program for childbearing teens, I found myself particularly drawn to Chapter 7. This chapter addresses the multiplicity of challenges, ranging from individual work loads to organizational issues, that direct service providers face. Deep care and concern for their clients are driving forces for most of them. Chapters 8 and 9 offer the reader a unique opportunity to appreciate the perspectives of program administrators and policy makers. Administrators face the formidable tasks of establishing programs, maintaining funding, developing community and interagency collaboration, and responding to specific programmatic concerns. Policy makers find themselves in the challenging position of forming a bridge between the needs of teen parents and service providers and the political infrastructure.

Adolescent Parenthood and Education: Exploring Alternative Programs is important because it turns our attention (particularly in the final chapters) to the pressing need for further analysis and research, examining service provision in the context of contemporary social debates: welfare, health care, and education reform; immigration; cultural and religious diversity; and degree of government involvement in the lives of citizens. The results of each of these debates, along with others surrounding abortion and male responsibility, will significantly influence the willingness of communities to provide appropriate services for childbearing teens, their partners, and their families.

We are living in a rapidly changing social climate. As Dr. Pilat so aptly points out, "Pregnant and parenting teenagers are today's lightning rod that seems to attract the emotional, psychological, and metaphysical concerns of the general population." There are still those who would blame teen mothers for all of the ills facing our society, rather than understanding that the lives of our young people are the *result*, not the cause, of social ills. In contrast to such negative views, Pilat provides clear and cogent direction for the provision of effective services for adolescent parents. Her work makes a distinct contribution to the efforts of those of us who are concerned with the well-being of America's young people and the future of our communities.

Catherine Monserrat, Ph.D.

Acknowledgments

Working with pregnant and parenting teens and their families has been a challenging yet rewarding experience. Their frank and open dialogue is the cornerstone of this work. I gratefully acknowledge the young parents and their families for sharing their stories. I am also grateful to the service providers, administrators, and policymakers who discussed their work, their concerns, and their visions of service-delivery systems, which enrich the lives of young parents.

In particular I would like to thank Grace, Jim, Lou, and Carol and editors Linda Jackson and Deborah Starewich. They each contributed to this work in unique and important ways.

Introduction

The purpose of this book is to provide a kaleidoscopic view of educational programs for pregnant and parenting teens. These educational programs have various components and organizational and individual stakeholders; they are dynamic systems. Just as the view through a kaleidoscope changes with every change in position, so one's view of a service-delivery system depends on the position/viewpoint of the participants and other stakeholders. Capturing the dynamic, vital activity of providing services to pregnant and parenting teens is as challenging as trying to describe the ever changing view created by a kaleidoscope.

Five alternative education models are examined in the following pages. All the models center around services to assist pregnant and parenting teens in completing their high school education. The models have academic educational components to which additional services are connected. The models differ, among other things, in governance, focus, and comprehensiveness of service. The models described in this book fall within a continuum of services to pregnant and parenting teens. Existing programs, some of which are within the categories described here, vary greatly and often combine different aspects of several programs. The categories presented here are offered for purposes of discussion and may be used by local school districts and other organizations as springboards for creating specific programs designed to meet community needs.

If trying to describe the various models of educational services for pregnant and parenting teens is like trying to describe chameleons viewed through a kaleidoscope, naming each model has been equally challenging. The relationship of the adolescent's local school district to the program offered is used as the basis for distinguishing among the many varieties of academic programs for pregnant and parenting teens. Based on this distinction, the five models of alternative education services to pregnant and parenting teens are as follows:

1. Alternative school
2. Cooperative school
3. Community-based program
4. Tutoring program
5. In-school program

These models, which are defined and compared in chapter 12, are an initial attempt to sort through and categorize a complex web of grass-roots services and programs that provide educational services to pregnant and parenting teenage women.

In this book I choose to view the service-delivery system from the various perspectives of its stakeholders, and in doing so, I make an effort to bridge the gap between research and practice. As a result, this book is presented to a variety of audiences. Not only may researchers find the methodology interesting and somewhat provocative in that a single case study is presented from a variety of perspectives, but it is also hoped that pregnant and parenting teens and their families and friends may find solidarity and support in the voices of their counterparts presented here. Direct-service providers, a crucial link in a service-delivery system, may find their own concerns articulated in the words of the service providers interviewed. Administrators and policymakers may recognize the complexity associated with planning, implementing, and evaluating programs for pregnant teens. Students in social work, public policy, counseling, and education will find concrete examples of client concerns and program management methods that may be useful in their training discussions. Some readers may find something to disagree with, while others may find new insights into the complex issues of service delivery. It is hoped that all readers will use this book as part of their continuing assessment of services for pregnant and parenting adolescents and their families.

My attempt at reaching a large and diverse audience entails bringing together the many perspectives of a variety of professions involved in the issues of adolescent pregnancy and parenting. I realize that by choosing to present a broad picture for a broad audience, the depth of detail may be missing for some individuals. However, through my experiences with pregnant and parenting teen mothers, their family and friends, and other stakeholders and through my research, I am convinced that it is essential to view the issues related to teenage pregnancy in their broad, complex, interprofessional, and real-life context.

Part 1 of this book presents two perspectives. Chapter 1 contains stories from my experience as a practitioner in the field of teenage pregnancy and parenting. In chapter 2 I describe the qualitative research methodology used in my 1990–91 study of a comprehensive alternative school for pregnant and parenting teens.

The study is more fully discussed in Part 2, which presents the perspectives of the various stakeholder groups involved in the issues of adolescent pregnancy. In chapter 3, I place the research project within a historical context and within its national, state, regional, and local settings. In chapter 4, I describe the Alternative Education Center for Young Mothers (AECYM), a comprehensive alternative school for pregnant and parenting teens. In chapters 5 through 9, I present the viewpoints of teen mothers, their support people, direct-service providers, administrators, and policymakers, respectively. In chapter 10, I present the results of the study.

In Part 3, I describe the five educational models for pregnant and parenting teens, and I base my description on my experience first as a teacher and then as a coordinator of a cooperative education program for pregnant and parenting teens. In chapter 11, I present a general discussion of alternative education. In chapter 12, I compare the five models of alternative programs, and in chapter 13, I present a portrait from practice and describe the issues that the various stakeholders in my program faced.

In Part 4, I describe recent trends and integrate them with the insights I have gained from practice.

As I—a practitioner and, more recently, a researcher—looked at various service-delivery models and listened to the views of the service-delivery system voiced by the various stakeholders, a focal point emerged: Adolescent parenting is not a problem to be solved but a reality to be lived. Programs and policies that enhance the ability of teen parents to live their lives in caring environments are appropriate models of service delivery. Creating such protective, supportive environments and communities is difficult and challenging, as the stakeholders will describe in the following pages.

Part I

Bridging the Gap between Research and Practice

Chapter One
A Practitioner's Perspective

From 1979 to 1988 I was coordinator of a cooperative education program for teenage girls who were pregnant, parenting, or both. During this time I learned that adolescent parenthood was a complex issue both for society and for the teens who were parents. Through my experiences with the young women in the program, their male partners, their parents and family members, and the professional service providers in the area, I came to realize that there are no easy solutions or quick fixes when one is dealing with the lives of young mothers and their children. Here are a few of their stories.

Joan's Story

Joan, a seventeen-year-old parent, had returned to the cooperative school for parenting teens in rural upstate New York just after giving birth to a baby girl. Joan began attending the alternative school in September, as soon as her pregnancy was confirmed. After only a few months, she had to remain in bed because of pregnancy complications. For four months before delivery a tutor visited twice a week. A bright student, Joan carried a full load of classes. All through her pregnancy Joan managed to keep up with her schoolwork. Now that she was returning to school, she had difficulty completing her assignments. One of the teachers suggested that perhaps Joan was spending too much time breast-feeding her child in the program nursery. The teacher suggested that perhaps Joan could use a breast pump and the child care attendant could feed her child so Joan could spend more time on her schoolwork.

Joan didn't buy that idea. "I can always take social studies over again," she said. "I'll never be able to feed her when she gets older." Joan dropped social studies.

Had we succeeded or failed as an alternative program for this student? Were her needs being met? How would this affect the school district's evaluation of the program? Here was another student dropping a course. On the other hand, wasn't she demonstrating fine parenting skills?

As the coordinator of the program, I had to ask these questions. Joan was clear and articulate. She was choosing parenting over schoolwork, a choice applauded by some and abhorred by others. She was not the first one to speak to me about the joy of parenthood and the importance of being a good mother.

Cathy's Story

At age fourteen, Cathy was the second-youngest of eleven daughters, all of whom were pregnant by the age of fifteen. What was unusual about Cathy was that the father of her child was forty-two years old and her father's friend. Her father approved of the relationship. When asked to describe her hopes and aspirations, Cathy stated that she wanted to get married, stay home, and knit.

As a student in the cooperative school, Cathy attended rather regularly and was exposed for the first time to computers, cosmetology, retailing, and other vocational classes, as well as to students from nine different school districts. She had an opportunity to visit, among other parts of the school, the school store, greenhouse, and restaurant—all of which were operated by students.

One day the students in the program were invited to the student-operated restaurant. Students generally paid for their own lunches when eating at the restaurant. In this case I made other arrangements for payment. So in we went to the restaurant. Everyone ordered, ate, and talked. During lunch Cathy thanked me for bringing her to the restaurant. It was the second time she had been in a restaurant in her life. Since Cathy called the student-operated restaurant a "real restaurant," I asked her what her first restaurant experience had been. Cathy told me that she had stopped at a fast-food place on a trip the previous summer.

After Cathy delivered her child, I made several home visits for tutoring purposes. As soon as I would pull up in the driveway, Cathy would come to the car window and tell me that she had to go somewhere or the baby was sick or she would give some other reason why I couldn't enter the house. She would hand me her work and take her next assignment. We would schedule another visit.

As I drove away, I was glad that she did not want me to come in. The ground around the house was muddy, with no sidewalk or driveway. The yard was strewn with parts from old washing machines, cars, and other mechanical devices, with perhaps a few antiques. The view from the car was of a porch filled with stacks of boxes, and every window appeared blocked with a stack of something. A German shepherd was chained to the front entrance.

During one visit, Cathy told me she was getting married. She would not be going back to school. A few years later, I met Cathy again. She was attending one of the general equivalency diploma (GED) classes at the vocational school. She now had three children.

Had we failed Cathy when she dropped out of school? Or did we succeed by giving her an option when she wanted to return to school? What happened to her three children? Could we have offered her other options while she was in the program? Had the environment and activities of the program created a dissonance for Cathy between her aspirations and the realities of her life?

Vivian's Story

Vivian was fourteen when she first came to the cooperative school. She was pregnant and engaged to a seventeen-year-old youth who worked on his parents' farm. By the end of the school year Vivian was married and living in a trailer on her in-laws' farm. By the end of her second year at the school, she was pregnant again and living in another trailer on property that she and her husband rented and used to raise dairy cattle. By the end of five years Vivian was divorced, had three children, and had moved south to a different state to live with her mother.

Pam's Story

Pam was seventeen, pregnant, and married to a nineteen-year-old man. Within a year, her husband was diagnosed with a rare form of cancer, her child became ill, and she herself became ill with pneumonia-like symptoms. She decided to drop out of school to care for her husband and daughter.

Sharri's Story

Sharri had been in the cooperative school for two years. She began attending during her sophomore year when she was pregnant, and she returned for her junior year with her child. She was now pregnant with her second child. While Sharri focused on schoolwork, her child was enrolled in the day care program. Sharri lived on a farm with her boyfriend, who had taken a job as a farmhand. With the job came living quarters. One day Sharri stepped off the school bus with her two-year-old daughter and all the paraphernalia needed for a two-year-old, as well as her books and school materials. In addition, she arrived with a large plastic garbage can in tow. Pulling this awkward thing behind her, she approached me. Could she do her laundry in the school washing machines that were used by the cosmetology class? Her washing machine was broken; she had no transportation to get her to a laundromat. She and her boyfriend did not own a car and did not have money to pay for a taxi to take them to the laundromat, which was their usual arrangement.

As an administrator/direct-service provider, I was interested in providing service for this young woman, so I agreed. Sharri could wash her clothes in the industrial-size washing machines used by several classes at the vocational school site that housed the alternative educational program Sharri attended. Little did I realize the questions this decision would raise from a variety of people, including school board members, teachers, parents, and administrators:

- Why was Sharri living with her boyfriend in the first place?
- Where were her parents?
- How could she ask for special treatment and additional services? She was already attending a school that provided day care and catered to her needs. How could she expect more?
- Was there an existing policy regarding personal use of the laundry facilities?
- Should the schools be in the business of providing laundry facilities for any group or individual?
- If the school allowed an individual to do personal laundry at school, would the school be taking business away from the local laundromats?
- What other options did Sharri have?

- Did helping a client get laundry done fall under the jurisdiction of comprehensive delivery of service to pregnant and parenting teens?
- What kinds of policies would help teen mothers to get their laundry done?
- What were the financial costs involved in laundering clothes?
- How did not having access to laundry facilities affect a teenage mother's ability to get and hold a job?

The Need for Answers

For those who work with pregnant and parenting teens, these are not unusual stories or simplistic questions. These and similar questions, and the answers to them, drive the implementation of service delivery at the client-provider level and directly affect the lives of pregnant and parenting teens and their families. The answers to these questions also drive the policymaking and administration of social programs that affect the lives of the service providers and administrators working with these teens. These stories and questions prompted me to leave my job as coordinator of the cooperative education program in 1988 after nine years so that I could pursue a career in research. Almost every day while I worked with teen mothers, new questions arose about the ethics of service, the best way to assist clients, client needs, and the support systems for the teens, their partners, their family members, and even the professionals who work with these young women.

In addition to my job as coordinator, I was president of a statewide organization of professional service providers who worked with pregnant and parenting adolescents and their families, and I therefore had the opportunity to interact with individuals from a variety of disciplines and representing a wide range of organizations. Issues of interagency cooperation and organizational participation in collaborative efforts at comprehensive service delivery and community networking surfaced during conferences with other professionals interested in the issue of adolescent pregnancy and parenting.

To answer some of these questions—better yet, to frame them—I decided to study a single-service delivery system to pregnant and parenting teens. I sought a place where I could observe but not be responsible for the daily operations of a program. I was graciously received as a participant observer at an alternative education program for pregnant and parenting teens in another city. I spent the spring of 1990 both meeting with various individuals who were involved with this alternative school and observing and interacting within the school setting and the service-delivery system. Using this in-depth ethnographic technique, I began to explore the dynamics of a service-delivery system in a systematic way.

As a result of this study and my previous work with pregnant and parenting teens, I arrived at my motto: Adolescent parenting is not a problem to be solved but a reality to be lived. Some teenagers who are raising children come to the realization that there are many problems associated with parenting but also many joys. It is the lives of these young women and their children and families that the service providers and the service-delivery system are dealing with. The purpose of the service-delivery system is to assist these families in solving the problems they encounter in caring for themselves and their children.

This may be viewed as an idealistic and somewhat naive approach to service delivery. However, recent research (Beck 1994; Noddings 1984, 1988, 1989, 1992, 1995) has shown that a caring environment is essential to healthy development. Treating individuals as problems is contrary to this caring, developmental approach.

While I was preparing this book and reporting on the findings of my research from the perspectives of the various stakeholders, a question arose. What was my perspective? Where did I stand? Was I a practitioner? researcher? administrator? How could I best articulate the bridge between research and practice, which I had been attempting to blend throughout my life? Using the first-person, singular voice seems to be the appropriate perspective, since the information in these pages is based on eighteen years of involvement with issues associated with teenage pregnancy and parenting, and my last six years of research have been based on the first twelve of direct service. As a result, my perspective consists of a continuing dialogue between experience and research.

Chapter Two
A Researcher's Perspective

Although I was interested in exploring service-delivery systems to pregnant and parenting teens and their families, designing a research study was much more difficult than summoning the desire to do one. Michael Knapp summarizes the difficulties of studying these systems.

The difficulty for those who wish to study comprehensive, collaborative services, however labeled, stems from their complexity and flexibility, the nature of collaborative effort, and the convergence of different disciplines. . . . Finally, the act of studying such endeavors engages researchers from traditions that do not normally communicate with one another. (Knapp 1995, 5)

In 1990 Dr. Knapp's insights were not available to guide me in designing the study, the results of which are described in Part 2. My first decision was to determine the type of research method to be used. I chose to conduct a qualitative study of an alternative education center for young parents that was based in a Northeastern urban community, and had outreach services to surrounding suburban and rural areas.

The choice of a qualitative study was based on Marshall's (1985) criteria for the appropriateness of qualitative method. Marshall's criteria are listed as follows:

- *Criterion:* Experimental research cannot be done for practical or ethical reasons. *Application:* The sheer size of the service-delivery system and the inability to control all the factors (e.g., cost and time) involved in such a system made it impossible for me to conduct an experimental study.

- *Criterion:* The research delves in depth with complexities and processes. *Application:* The research study needed to explore a complex service-delivery system to parenting adolescents, including such processes as referral, funding, program planning and implementation, and policy development.
- *Criterion:* Relevant variables and interconnections have yet to be identified and described. *Application:* A significant part of the work had to explore relationships: (1) between individuals, (2) between organizations, and (3) between individuals and organizations. Describing the dynamics of these relationships, the connections, and variables would be central to the study.
- *Criterion:* The research seeks to understand instances where policy, folk wisdom, and current practice do not work. *Application:* The study required an analysis of the policies and practices of a current service-delivery system, to determine if it was working, how it was working, and what were the barriers to or enhancers of successful service.
- *Criterion:* The research is on unknown societies or innovative systems. *Application:* Service-delivery systems to pregnant and parenting teens, although available for years, had not been extensively explored as dynamic systems and were therefore innovative systems.
- *Criterion:* The research is on informal and unstructured linkages and processes in organizations. *Application:* Of particular interest in this study was the informal networking system among clients, service providers, and other interested individuals and groups.
- *Criterion:* The research seeks to explore a central phenomenon from a variety of theoretical perspectives. *Application*: An examination of the service-delivery system needed to be grounded in organizational, educational, and sociological theory, among others.
- *Criterion:* The research seeks a subjective understanding of individuals. *Application:* I planned to study the service-delivery system from the viewpoints of the various individuals involved in the system, including pregnant and parenting

teens, their families and support people, direct-service providers, administrators, and policymakers.

Design and Implementation

Having settled on a qualitative aproach to studying a service-delivery system to pregnant and parenting teens, I divided the research into two phases: Phase 1 was the national context, and Phase 2 was the local context (see appendix A). Phase 1 consisted of an examination of the concerns national policymakers had regarding adolescent pregnancy and parenting and helped to frame the research study. Phase 1 included (*a*) six formal and six informal interviews with national policymakers at the 1989 annual meeting of a national professional organization devoted to adolescent pregnancy issues in Washington, D.C. (see appendix B for the protocol for interviews with policymakers) and (*b*) a review of archival material such as legislative bills and minutes of congressional hearings (see appendix C).

Phase 2 of this research, based on the findings of the phase 1 interviews, was conducted in three stages at a local service-delivery site chosen by the following criteria:

1. The primary service-delivery agency was a school-based program.
2. The community in which the primary agency operated was a racially integrated community.
3. The school-based program selected needed to provide a wide range of services either directly or through a referral system.

In stage 1 of this phase community demographics were compiled and key variables associated with school attendance and with the availability of, access to, and use of services were determined through a review of documents (see appendix C).

Stage 2 consisted of individual and group interviews with forty teenage mothers and thirteen support people, including families and friends (see appendix D for data sheets for clients and family support). These interviews were conducted in homes, schools, places of employment, and other convenient locations. Additional information from teenage mothers resulted from the administration of a questionnaire developed in collaboration with me by the pregnant and parenting teenagers who attended the civics class of the alternative education center (see appendix E). The purpose of the questionnaire was to reach students who were part of the school's outreach program and who could not attend the alternative education center.

Stage 3 included interviews with twenty-one direct-service providers (see appendix F for the protocol for interviews with service providers) and seventeen program administrators (see appendix G for the protocol for interviews with program administrators). Extensive notes were taken during the six weeks spent in the field as a participant observer in the spring of 1990. Observational notes (appendix H) were taken on the interactions that took place at the local agencies where services were provided to the parenting teens. During these visits to local agencies documents, reports, and informational materials were gathered and reviewed. Transcripts of taped interviews were analyzed and themes categorized through the use of Hyper Research computer software.

Individual and group interviews with teen mothers, their support persons, and family members were conducted. Interviews were also conducted with direct-service providers, those professionals who work directly with clients such as teachers, social workers, counselors, and nurses. Program administrators and local policymakers were also interviewed.

Most interviews were audiotaped; when this was not possible, I took handwritten notes. I also recorded my reflections and observations. When I visited the various programs that were part of the service-delivery system, I collected their brochures, pamphlets, annual reports, and other documents and records.

My initial contact with the service-delivery system was made through the director of the alternative school, whom I had known professionally for a number of years. During the first day at the school, the director introduced me to the students and explained that I was interested in seeing how the school operated and would therefore be spending several weeks there meeting with students, their partners, friends, families, teachers, etc. At that first meeting the researcher asked for volunteers for individual interviews and asked the teens to identify primary-support individuals whom I might also interview.

As with any research project, problems emerged. Working with parenting teens presented several specific problems, particularly that of parental permission. Emancipated minors who (regardless of age) were heads of their own households did not need parental permission to be interviewed. However, any student (regardless of age) living with a parent or guardian did need parental permission to be interviewed. An exception to this arose when a student adjudicated as an emancipated minor was living at home and paying rent to her parents. I interviewed her on her own authority. This issue of parental permission for research purposes is somewhat disconcerting, given the fact that the teen mother, regardless of age, is legally responsible for her own child. This tension between parental authority and personal responsibility for one's self and one's child is an interesting and powerful dynamic that emerges in interviews with both parenting teens and their parents.

Another research problem surfaced when I began to seek out the individuals who provided support to the parenting teen. Asking the teen mothers to identify their primary support person was easy; trying to make contact with that support person was challenging. Often the support people were hesitant to talk with me because they feared that I was somehow connected with Social Services, the Internal Revenue Service, or some other government agency and that I was in some way trying to evaluate or monitor their income and activities for punitive purposes. Gradually this stigma was overcome, thanks to the trust and kindness of the staff of the alternative school. When the girls saw the director, faculty, and staff of the alternative school interact with me trustingly, the girls themselves began to trust me. Without that support, I would never have been able to contact the teen mothers' primary support persons.

Participants in the individual interviews were given $5 gift certificates for participating in the interviews and for returning their parental permission slips. This proved an effective tool in recruiting teen mothers for individual interviews. In addition to interviewing them, I had ample time to observe and interact with the young women throughout the day (in their classes, in the day care center with their children, and in the cafeteria) while I was at the alternative school. The researcher also had the opportunity to visit with several of the teen mothers and their families in their homes.

The individual and group interviews with direct-service providers, program administrators, and local policymakers were usually conducted in their offices. This gave me the opportunity to observe the various organizational settings in which the teenage mothers received services and to get a sense of the conditions in the community.

A Word about Teen Fathers

Only teen mothers attended the Alternative Education Center for Young Mothers; therefore the teen mothers were interviewed first. I then asked the teen mothers to help me contact the fathers, but in most cases the teen mothers were no longer involved with the father of their child. I therefore interviewed whomever the teen mother indicated was her male partner at the time. Many teen mothers no longer had a significant male partner, and some of those who had one did not want him to be interviewed. Since the teen mother was the nodal point around which the services in this system were delivered, I viewed the teen mother's male partner, friends, and family members as support people.

Assumptions and Limitations

When I chose to focus on the service-delivery system broadly rather than in minute detail, several assumptions and limitations were revealed.

- *Determination of needs.* When services were reviewed from the clients' perspective, they were asked whether they needed particular services such as food, clothing, and health care. If they did not need a particular service, they were asked if they knew where to obtain it if they needed it. The limitation to this approach was that knowing where to obtain the services does not necessarily mean that services are adequate. However, it is an indication that clients are aware of the service and at least have a starting point in any effort to secure services when needed. The other concern in determining need from the client's perspective is whether the clients are the best judges of their own needs. Even though the clients in these cases were teenagers, this research is based on the assumption that clients are, if not the best judge of their own needs, very good judges. When these needs are viewed from their own perspective and taken into consideration with the needs of the other stakeholders in the service-delivery system, a broad view of the adequacy of services can be portrayed.

- *Teen participants.* The pregnant and parenting adolescents interviewed or surveyed during this study were in some way connected with the Alternative Education Center for Young Mothers. They either attended the center's alternative education program or were part of its outreach program. The limitation to this was that other teen mothers in the community were not interviewed. However, the center reaches a majority of the pregnant teens in the community, and in addition to the teenage mothers, direct-service providers from other agencies in the community were interviewed. In this way, the issues facing the clients not connected with the center were somewhat articulated.

- *Identification of support individuals.* To identify individuals who were of support to the pregnant and parenting teens, I relied on the input of the clients, and this could be perceived as a limitation. Support has different meanings to different people. Support may mean financial support, moral support, or provision of food, clothing, shelter, etc. Whom the client identified depended on the client's interpretation of support. The support people in turn identified the support they received, or lack thereof, based on their understanding of support. The results of the interviews with the support people are reported in chapter 6.

Part II

Study of a Comprehensive Alternative Education System for Pregnant and Parenting Teens

Chapter Three
The Setting

The relationship between a single individual and a service-delivery system is meaningful not only to the client for whom the services are intended but also to other individuals in her family, in various other organizations within her community, and in society. This gradually expanding relationship between one teenager and the system is far more complex than can be described "by the most creative amalgam of thinking and imagination" (Sarason 1972, xiii). Through a description of settings and subsystems within the local service-delivery system, the complexities of service delivery emerge.

This description provides a backdrop for the voices of the various stakeholders involved in the service-delivery system and thus reflects a more holistic representation of the life of a parenting teen in the service-delivery system.

In this chapter I provide a background for the Alternative Education Center for Young Mothers (AECYM). I begin with a wide-angle view of the national setting and gradually focus on smaller geopolitical regions.

It is important to note that this setting was not static but rather dynamic. While this study was taking place, changes in policies, programs, and life circumstances were underway. Because of this dynamic aspect, the following summary of the setting represents only a limited view of the service-delivery system during the spring of 1990. As in chapter 1, this chapter includes a few anecdotes that help to frame the issues that were addressed by the research.

National Setting

During lunch at the annual conference of a national professional organization focused on adolescent pregnancy issues, a director for a community service project was discussing with eight of us her dismay over a certain funding regulation. "No wonder it's so difficult to get funding. Even the Pope would have difficulty—well maybe not the Pope, but surely most responsible organizations." The director was referring to a regulation that prohibited use of federal funds for any program that was in any way associated with abortion, even the mention of abortion. A federal employee in an office responsible for funding responded that this strict regulation was indeed a barrier to funding adolescent pregnancy services and prevention programs but, as an employee of the federal government, she was obliged to follow such regulations.[1]

This scenario presents two points about the service-delivery system at the national setting. First, even employees at the highest levels of service delivery are caught in the unenviable position of knowing that a regulation is a barrier to service but being obliged to see that the regulation is implemented.

Second, the remarks demonstrate the ongoing national controversy over the issue of abortion and the impact this has on teenage pregnancy and parenting services. Federal, state, and local funds for teenage pregnancy programs are often contingent upon the exclusion of abortion in family planning, counseling, and referral. While the issues surrounding the abortion controversy are varied and complex and not the direct subject of this study, it is clear that the AECYM is involved in this controversy.

The center, which discussed all forms of family planning, including abortion, and referred clients to, and received referrals from, the local family planning organization, was therefore not eligible for direct federal funding. Although most AECYM clients have already decided to continue the pregnancy before coming to the center, the director of the center nonetheless needed to walk a fine line in this abortion controversy.

National Update
Since the conclusion of this study in 1991, the debate on abortion, teenage pregnancy and parenting, and the welfare system has intensified. Pregnant and parenting teens have become the second most vilified group in our society. The one group that surpasses them in public disgust are youth who commit violent crimes. I am

personally outraged that the public has turned on its youth with hostile and punitive attitudes at a time when crimes against children escalate.

A summary of the policy debate between welfare and adolescent pregnancy and parenting is provided in a January 1995 paper prepared for the North Central Extension directors of the Cooperative Extension Service and entitled "Welfare Reform and the Role of Extension Programming":

[W]hile the United States does have a teenage pregnancy problem it is also true that the context of this program is often not adequately appreciated and, as a consequence, that the policy actions pursued are ill-conceived and/or lead to unintended and undesirable consequences. . . . [W]hile it is the case that rates of unintended adolescent pregnancy remain unacceptably high—indeed, rates of adolescent pregnancy in the United States are higher than in any other industrialized nation, have increased over the past two decades and . . . one million adolescents become pregnant each year in the United States—the rate of pregnancy among teenagers who have had intercourse has actually declined. . . . [C]ontrary to popular belief, rates of adolescent childbearing declined from the mid-1950s through 1987, when the rates began to increase. . . . In fact, the 1992 rate of 61 live births per 1,000 adolescents is well below the corresponding rates that existed throughout the 1950s and 1960s. . . .

However . . . policymakers have become concerned with demographic trends in nonmarital adolescent childbearing. The birth rate for unmarried adolescents has doubled since 1970 . . . reaching—in 1992— a rate of 44.6 live births per 1,000 unmarried adolescents. . . . [P]olicy makers' interest in this trend in births to unmarried adolescents derives from the results of several analyses of the burden placed on the federal budget by adolescent childbearing, and particularly nonmarital childbearing. For example, a report by the Center for Population Options (1992) estimates that the 1990 single-year costs attributable to adolescent childbearing for three federal programs—AFDC, Food Stamps, and Medicaid—were approximately $25 billion! Moreover, Garfinkel and McLanahan (1986, 1994) indicate that the birth of a child to an unmarried adolescent mother increases the likelihood that she and her child will utilize programs such as AFDC. Indeed, Bane and Ellwood

(1986) found that, in 30% of the cases, the beginning of a spell on AFDC was associated with the birth of a first child to an unmarried woman. (Lerner, Bogenschneider, Wilcox, Fitzsimmons, and Cox Hoopfer 1995, 34)[2]

Based on this analysis, it is hoped when challenged by policy changes in this time of transition and uncertainty, service deliverers will show compassion and care for the individuals affected by the policy.

State Setting

Although the national setting has changed drastically since the completion of my field research, the state setting has remained relatively the same and the issues surrounding funding remain the same.

In a hotel lobby where the 1990 Annual State Family Life Conference was being held, several service providers were discussing recent state legislation.

One service provider said, "What good is this legislation making family life education and the community service projects part of the ongoing state budget if no funds are passed along with it? I hate this waiting."

Another responded, "At least we don't have to go through the legislative hearings every year, only the budget. That'll save some time."

The third service provider remarked, "It's hard trying to keep my people motivated while this process is going on. We must keep hanging in there waiting to hear. It's become almost a yearly ritual; some people are even starting to get used to it."

Comments such as these were common during the conference. During that spring, the state experienced one of the longest periods in its history without a state budget. Therefore, at the time of this research, program administrators, direct-service providers, and other agency personnel were unsure of continued funding for several programs that were part of the referral system for teen parents. Their jobs and their programs were in danger of being eliminated. This anxiety-producing situation was reflected in my conversations with program administrators and direct-service providers at the conference. Although legislation making family life education and services to pregnant and parenting teens part of the ongoing state budget was passed, a decision about the actual funding for these programs was not forthcoming.

This uncertainty was evident during a conversation I had with several social workers from a special unit of the Department of Social Services. Through this program, a separate team of case managers and income-maintenance workers at the department was authorized to oversee all services for parenting teens. This service was voluntary. Yet the number of clients requesting services within the first month was three times the projected yearly number. With the onset of the new program, the caseload of the social workers in this unit was cut in half and, therefore, these case workers could provide individual and thorough case management. Since each locality could develop its own plan for implementation, mixed reviews for the program were presented to the legislature. Although the program was seen as a tremendous asset in the studied service-delivery area, the future of the total program from the state perspective was uncertain at the time of this study.

The counselors at the AECYM were concerned with the state budgetary crisis as well. Their clients were referred to special social workers who provided access and guidance for parenting teens through the social service system. The clients also viewed the special social workers' team as an important referral. When asked, "Where would you refer a friend who was pregnant for services?" the second largest response by a group of seniors at the center was "The special social workers, they help you get everything you need."[3] If the state budget had been cut, the services of these special social workers would have been cut, leaving a large void in the service-delivery system. It is evident from this brief discussion of the state setting that the service-delivery system to pregnant and parenting teens at the local level is vulnerable to state-level fiscal policies. While the state budget may be a matter of monetary figures at the upper levels of management, individuals' lives are touched through the possible loss of their jobs or services.[4]

Regional Setting

The newspaper headline "Metro Bus, Rail Shut Down: Union Rejects Last Bid to Keep System Operating" greeted me the morning of my interview with the director of the regional youth bureau. Cognizant of the fact that the transit shutdown was a possibility, we had purposely scheduled the meeting for 9:30, assuming that the worst of the rush hour traffic would be over. To my surprise, traffic was light and I found the Executive Building easily. As we began our interview I learned that many people who normally used the transit system had stayed home from work. I wondered how many clients of the AECYM had stayed home from school.

Located in a large metropolitan, internationally accessible region of a northeastern state, the local service-delivery system was highly dependent on the transportation system of the neighboring county and metropolitan area. During the study, the bus and rail transportation systems originating in the next county and serving the local areas were shut down for lack of funds and because of charges of corruption and mismanagement.

At the AECYM, the impact on school attendance was minimal because most of the students used school district transportation or taxicabs or walked to school. However, the shutdown of the transportation system did have a major impact on pregnant and parenting teens who used public transportation for medical appointments, general shopping, and other needs. The shutdown of the transit system left many teen parents from rural areas (where taxi service is limited or nonexistent) without transportation. Although bus and rail transportation was restored within a few days, the short period without public transportation highlighted its importance to the service-delivery systems for pregnant or parenting teens.

Much of this regional scene has changed little since the time of my field research.

County Setting

As I stood in the hall of the AECYM, I watched one of the counselors balancing a briefcase, a stack of papers, a take-out dish of salad, and a diet soft drink as she attempted to open the door to the parking lot. This was a March day, so she also had her raincoat in hand. As I helped her open the door, she told me she was headed for an appointment with an outreach client in a rural area. It would take her between thirty and forty minutes to get there, so she thought she would save time and eat in the car.

Because the county is divided into two general areas (the urban western region and the rural eastern region), the AECYM operates an in-school program as well as an outreach program to rural areas. The alternative school itself is located in the western region in the city. According to the center's 1989 statistical report, 51.9 percent of births to teen mothers in the county occurred in the city and surrounding suburban communities. Of these young mothers, 68.5 percent resided in the census tracts with not only the highest rates of teenage pregnancy but also the highest rates of school dropouts, juvenile delinquency, unemployment, and single-parent families. The average age of the mothers of the pregnant teenagers (ages thirteen to fifteen) in those tracts was twenty-nine to thirty-one, indicating that they, too, had been teenage mothers.

The AECYM outreach program is geared to serving clients in the eastern region of the county, which is generally rural and contains a few small towns. Of the 217 adolescent mothers served through the outreach program, 88 percent were white, 9.7 percent were black, 0.04 percent were Native American, and 2.2 percent were Hispanic. Of the young mothers or their families 31.8 percent received public assistance, 27.2 percent received partial assistance (Aid to Dependent Children [ADC]), 1.4 percent received Social Security, and 38.6 percent were financially independent.

By providing both an in-school and an outreach program, the AECYM responded to the specific needs of both populations. However, this dual programming affects the implementation of services. Direct providers, administrators, and policymakers needed to consider time, mileage, and other travel costs, both financial and personal, when they incorporated outreach components into programs for pregnant and parenting teens.

Since the conclusion of my fieldwork, much of the county setting has changed little. There are no new transportation systems to assist counselors in traveling throughout the county.

City Setting

The following city scene could well take place today as during the time of my field research: Each morning, while driving to the AECYM, I passed chemical industrial complexes for a three-mile stretch of road along the river. A teen father I interviewed had just lost his job at one of these companies, and a former student of the center now worked for one. As I turned up a local street, the scene changed from industrial to residential. While driving the mile and a half from the chemical plants to the center, I recalled that the school district superintendent mentioned that 65 percent of the single mothers in the city lived within a mile radius of the center. What impact did the chemical industry have on health and unemployment?

The city has a population of approximately 70,000 residents, of whom 85 percent are white, 13 percent black, 1 percent Native American/Eskimo, and 1 percent Hispanic. Tourism, the chemical industry, and energy production are the chief businesses in the area. Statistics from the 1989 AECYM annual report revealed that the "steepest rise in teenage births has been among 16- to 19-year-old, low-income white girls."

The AECYM is located within the city limits and within one mile of 65 percent of all single family households in the city. The clients from the city proper and the western region of the county were 49 percent black, 49 percent white, and 2 percent other. Of the young mothers or their families 45.3 percent received public assistance, 5.6 percent received partial assistance (ADC), 3 percent received only Medicaid and food stamps, 3 percent received Social Security, 6 percent received Social Security and partial assistance (ADC), 3.4 percent received disability, and 33.7 percent were financially independent.

Summary

These descriptions of national, state, regional, county, and city settings add depth and dimension to the overall picture of service delivery to parenting teens. Concern about federal legislation at the national level, budgetary problems at the state level, transportation difficulties at the regional level, the geopolitical distribution of the population at the county level, and the economic condition of the city were some of the issues that influenced the service-delivery system during the spring of 1990.

Notes

1. All quotes, unless otherwise described, are from field notes.
2. For more information about the national debate, see Lerner (1995).
3. The greatest number of respondents recommended the AECYM as the place where one could send a friend who was pregnant.
4. The state experienced a similar fiscal crisis in 1995.

Chapter Four
The Alternative Education Center for Young Mothers

With regard to a service-delivery system to parenting adolescents, agreement on values and objectives seems rare. The nature of adolescent pregnancy taps the very heart of our biological, moral, social, and psychological being. Controversy over the best way for society to deal with adolescent pregnancy has been well documented (Lerner 1995; Compton, Duncan, and Hruska 1987; Hayes 1987; Vinovskis 1988). Because of this controversy, it was important for me to study a service-delivery system for which it appeared that agreement had been reached on the objectives of, if not the values for, the delivery of services to parenting teens. At the time of my study, the Alternative Education Center for Young Mothers (AECYM) had operated for over twenty years. The AECYM was the hub of the service-delivery system to pregnant and parenting teens at the local site, as figure 4.1 illustrates.

The AECYM was the nodal point around which the service-delivery system to parenting teens operated in the community. Services emanated from this educational setting, and day care and counseling were on site.[1] The counseling portion of the center was the conduit through which clients made contact with other services in the community such as health care, financial support, food and housing subsidies, and transportation. From the clients' perspective based on my interviews with them, the staff of this counseling program were the key to service delivery. The center's director provided the leadership and expertise that kept the channels of communication open among the various agencies that provided the services.

The concept, in which pregnant teens would be voluntarily enrolled in an alternative school, was developed at this local site during a two-year period twenty-five years ago. Previously tutors

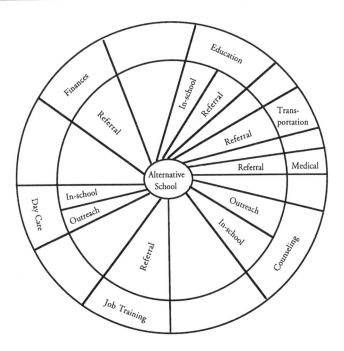

Figure 4.1. Alternative Education Center Wheel

had been sent to the homes of the pregnant students. This was time-consuming and often proved ineffective when the client had to return to the home school shortly after the birth of her child. At that time, little support was available for teen parents. After a year and a half of extensive research by a community advisory board, the school district provided a classroom, a teacher, a social worker, educational materials, and other support for the program. Under the leadership of the school district and the program director, the alternative school had evolved during its twenty-five-year history into its present comprehensive structure.

The education component always remained central to the system. Although controversy arose over the equity issues of separating pregnant teens from the rest of the student body, the pregnant and parenting teens at the center indicated during interviews that they preferred to be in a single-sex educational setting in which there were small classes, personalized attention, and courses specifically designed for their unique educational needs (such as parenting, budgeting, and child development). Although they missed some of the activities of their local high schools, almost all felt alienated and disenfranchised from them. They felt they had little in common with other students; their concerns centered around their children and parenting issues. They preferred to be with other girls who had similar concerns. They found the absence of males to be an asset, since it allowed them to concentrate on their schoolwork without having to worry about a male-female relationship during the school day. These attitudes may have been rationalizations on their part to cope with a crisis situation; nevertheless, the educational and counseling benefits of small class size and individual attention have achieved documented results in fostering increased school attendance, completion of high school, greater personal esteem, and better parenting skills. Some students did indicate that they would go back to their regular high school if day care and the individual attention they received at the AECYM could be provided there.

One student described the decision of whether to attend the regular school or the AECYM as one of a set of trade-offs that required her to think realistically about her situation. "It's really a privilege to attend the center. . . . You can get a diploma," she said. So why did she choose the center?

Well, if you have day care, it's a lot easier to go back to your own school, go to dances . . . but sometimes it's not allowed because of your situation. Here at the alternative school they give you close attention, show you child care, tell you what you need to know . . . they're patient and understanding. There is no difference in intelligence between those at the AECYM and others. We have all levels in some classes, you learn to be patient. . . . Teachers here are excellent and fair. Teachers make sure you know the information.

It is obvious from this quote that the student had struggled with, and had come to a realistic understanding of, her situation and how to make the most of it. She planned to attend college and at the time of the study was working as an aide in the main office of the center. Her comments made it clear that the day care and the knowledge of parenting that the school could provide were important to her. However, she left open the question of whether she would attend the regular school if day care were available on site at the high school. Day care is one of the most important issues in school attendance for the teen mother after the birth of her child.

At the AECYM, the day care component was directed by a registered nurse. The director of the school believed that a health background was essential to the overall operation of this component. Because of her health training, the day care coordinator could answer students' questions regarding the health of their children as well as conduct classes in child development, infant first aid, and parenting. She was also able to instruct and supervise the students in the proper administration of medication to their children.

Another unique feature of the day care component at the center was the use of paid foster grandparents as day care aides. The students themselves also assisted in the operation of the day care and were responsible for feeding their children at lunchtime. This intergenerational staff provided a positive atmosphere from which each generation benefitted. The foster grandparents stated that they enjoyed being with the children and helping the young mothers.

The alternative school operated an outreach program for pregnant and parenting teens in the eastern rural end of the county. This outreach component provided case management and referral services. The counselors also conducted support group meetings. Until recently, no educational programs had been available for these rural students unless they traveled to the western part of the county to attend the alternative school. In 1989, however, the Board of Cooperative Educational Services in the eastern county introduced an alternative educational program for pregnant teens in their areas. The alternative school provided group counseling sessions for students who attended the Eastern Region Alternative Education Program.

As shown in figure 4.2, auxiliary services were available to the clients of the AECYM through a referral network.

Referral Network

During 1989 the staff at the AECYM contacted other agencies over 3,700 times regarding services for their pregnant and parenting teen clients (Center for Young Parents 1990). The alternative school had working agreements and referral systems with over fifty public and

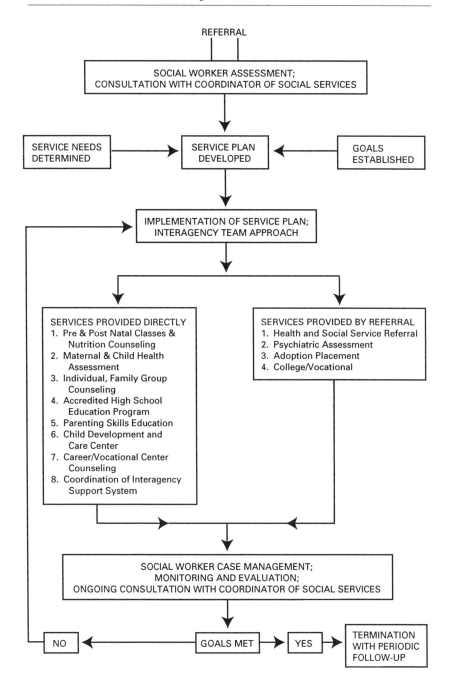

Figure 4.2. Client Flow Chart

private agencies. Once clients had been referred to the AECYM, the social worker, in consultation with the coordinator of social services, conducted an assessment of the needs of the client. Individual clients, together with the alternative school counselors, established individual goals and developed a service plan. Periodic reassessment with the teen parent was conducted and follow-up services were provided.

Most service providers from outside agencies felt that the social workers at the alternative school were excellent case managers for the clients, they eagerly referred pregnant and parenting adolescents to the center. Reciprocally, social workers at the center did not hesitate to refer clients to outside agencies for additional services.

Positive and supportive comments were the norm in 98 percent of my conversations with clients, service providers, family support personnel, and program administrators concerning the referral system available to parenting teens. Even when these people were specifically asked to discuss the barriers to referral, positive comments prevailed. Based on observational and client interview data, the referral system was very effective in meeting the needs of teen parents enrolled in the alternative school and its outreach components.

According to those interviewed, informality, size, and nonduplication of services were the components that accounted for the success of the referral system.

Informality

Most of the staff in agencies within the referral system knew each other on a first-name basis. All but one of the program administrators, and most of the direct-service providers, felt they could call their respective contact persons and easily make a referral that would culminate in services for the client. The ability of the direct-service providers to contact each other and refer to each other by name was mentioned as an important factor in service delivery.

Size

Several interviewees stated that this informality was possible because of the size of the local area served and the relatively low client/staff ratio at each agency, compared to the client/staff ratio in larger metropolitan areas. Also the number of staff people assigned to work with the parenting teens in each agency was relatively small. In many cases the same person handled all the parenting teen clients within a given agency. One program administrator discussed how a case manager and small caseload could overcome a client's inhibitions about using the system:

Some teens are inhibited coming into a bureaucracy because they don't know who they're going to see (in some agencies you never see the same person twice in a row). Clients might ask questions such as "What floor is my case worker on this week?" "Who do I see?" Case management and small caseloads are a means of counteracting these concerns in this local service-delivery system.

Nonduplication of Services

A discussion arose as to the meaning of duplication. Does duplication of services exist in this community if more than one program provides the same service? If two organizations provide the same service, are they actually the same service or do nuances in organizational philosophy provide options rather than duplication? One program administrator, describing the overlap in the parenting programs available from different organizations, summed up the discussion this way:

There's a lot of overlapping of services (in a sense, I think you would say it was duplication) . . . there are several agencies that do parenting programs, for example. I never feel like that means I should discontinue our program, because I think that it's helpful for people to be able to choose if they want to work with this agency or that one.

The issue of options is especially important in controversial areas in which the values of an organization play an important part in the services offered. Program administrators did not see a parenting program offered by Planned Parenthood and one offered by Catholic Charities as a duplication; the administrators felt that different clients would use different services. Duplication exists when different organizations are competing for the same clients and providing the same services. In this study, the discussion of duplication is mostly theoretical because very few organizations within the service-delivery system studied offered similar programs.

In the local service-delivery system, referrals operated effectively because they were informal and had manageable caseloads and little duplication of services. The providers who made the referrals knew each other by name. In addition, the sharing of information in orientation sessions for new providers conducted at the AECYM, on-the-job training, and regular personal contact among the service providers were keys to the success of the referral network.

Funding Network

During 1989 the alternative school was funded by the school district; local and county United Way agencies; local, county, and state youth boards; and the local Department of Youth and Recreation (see figure 4.3). In-kind contributions were provided by the Department of Public Health and the Foster Grandparents program. The fiscal management of the alternative school was an excellent example of creative programming and fiscal accountability.

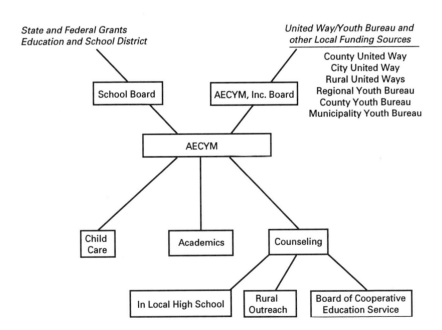

Figure 4.3. Funding Sources

The academic, in-school component of the alternative school was funded through the local school district. This funding included administrative and teacher salaries and fringe benefits as well as rent, maintenance, and utility expenses. The center was located in a community education center that was owned by the school district and that housed other community programs such as Head Start, job training programs, Adult Basic Education, and other alternative education programs.

However, the outreach, counseling, and child care components of the program were funded by other sources through an incorporation mechanism. By being incorporated as a not-for-profit agency, the AECYM could accept outside funds that were not normally allocated to school districts. This funding strategy allowed the AECYM to operate its outreach programs in other parts of the county. Funds came to the AECYM directly through the school district, from outside sources such as United Way with the school district acting as a fiscal agent, or directly through the corporation.

Another funding strategy unique to this geographical area was the joint application process used by the United Ways of the region and the regional Division for Youth. These were the two umbrella funding sources for the majority of the not-for-profit agencies in the region. Several years before the study, the directors of these funding agencies had devised a joint application process. It allowed each agency requesting funds to submit only one application to all the regional and local United Ways and youth bureaus (seven in total). This process eliminated bureaucratic paperwork and allowed each agency requesting funds to make a single presentation before all the funding sources. At the same time, the funding agencies maintained autonomous decision-making powers. As one agency director commented:

By merging those [processes] you get the best of both worlds or the best of all worlds, really. To sit in that appeal or that session, you are hearing different questions that might trigger other thoughts in your mind. So you're not only making efficient use of volunteers' time and agency time, but by getting those different perspectives, we really feel you've developed a good situation.

This process was viewed very favorably by all the program administrators interviewed. In one case, the director of the funding agency sought additional information from the funded agencies through site visits conducted by her staff. The program administrators commented that the site visits were not disruptive of the funding process, and all the program administrators stated that joint funding applications saved time and were a positive strategy. As a result of this process, a network of funded agencies that met regularly to discuss the emerging needs of the community existed.

Once again, face-to-face contact gave program administrators (whose programs served many of the same clients) an opportunity to know each other personally and to discuss common concerns and programming needs. The dynamic interplay of all these components created the service-delivery system that operated out of the AECYM.

Summary

The service-delivery system that centered around the AECYM—

- Served pregnant and parenting teens through on-site academic classes, child care, and counseling services.
- Served additional pregnant and parenting teens through counseling sessions, informational meetings, and other outreach activities in traditional high schools, community centers, and vocational schools.
- Provided, through a referral network with other community agencies, services that were not available on site or through outreach activities.
- Used a referral system that was formalized through linkage agreements and yet was small enough for service providers to know each other by name.
- Received assistance from the school district that provided the building and utilities and funded the teachers' salaries and other academic activities.
- Received additional funds that were provided through grants, with the school acting as the fiscal agent.
- Allowed the incorporation of the AECYM, enabled the AECYM to act as fiscal agent for activities geographically and legally outside the service of the school district.

Note

1. Service-delivery systems to pregnant and parenting teens vary as to their arrangement and include such models as single-site, hospital-based programs and multisite, community-based referral systems.

Chapter 5
The Voice of
Adolescent Parents

Bright, articulate, and responsible were three words that described Jamie. I met Jamie on my first day at the education center and after a general meeting, during which I was introduced by the center's director and then explained my purpose and asked for volunteers for interviews. Immediately following this presentation, Jamie approached me with her consent form in hand, and she was willing and eager to tell her story. As an emancipated minor, Jamie, who was pregnant at age fifteen, now lived alone with her son and, at the age of seventeen, was legally responsible for herself.

However, it wasn't until three weeks later that I was able to interview her formally. Although we had made several appointments to get together, something always "came up." She was absent from school for two days because of her sick child; another day she left early for a doctor's appointment and needed to use her study hall time to catch up on her academic assignments and work schedule. She conscientiously informed me of all these changes and cancellations. During those three weeks I had the opportunity to observe Jamie interact in several classes, work as a student intern in the main office, and interact with her child. When we finally met and I asked her to describe her life, Jamie made the following comments:

I lived at home when I was pregnant. Transportation was a problem 'cause my dad works and my mom don't drive and I had to go to the doctor, and when it was bad out, I had to walk ten blocks. I was on Medicaid when I was pregnant, but I didn't know if they provided transportation. The doctors treated me nicely, but at church they weren't going to baptize my baby because you either had to belong to a church or you had to be married. The church shouldn't be prejudiced against my age or my status of not being married. You know, I still have a baby, and it still has to be baptized. I went to a different church. This one was going to baptize him. It's hard because I don't have a relationship with the baby's father. I just see him when he sees the baby. He goes out with the baby when he's not working. I don't get much time out, I don't get much recreation, because I don't have a baby-sitter. My mom, she has a bad back, so she can't really take care of him. My sister has three kids of her own and goes to school. She went back to college, so I don't really go anywhere after school, outside of school, unless I take my son with me. Sometimes I go to visit my mom, [go to] a friend's house, go to the store, to the park, or something. I wish I could just get a break sometimes. Like when vacations come up, I'll be with my son for two weeks. He won't get away from me, and I won't get away from him. We'll only get one break from each other, when he goes to bed, and then I'll stay up. I wish I had someone to baby-sit, you know, someone good that knows how to handle kids. Just to go for a walk, or something. I'd have the money to pay a baby-sitter if I was still working in school.

Another thing: I can't have a phone 'cause I'm not eighteen. The phone company refuses to—said it was their policy. I had asked my counselor to try, my social worker to try, and I tried, and they all said it was against their policy to give me a phone because of my age, because I was not eighteen years old. I told them my son was sickly; he gets ear infections. They refused to give me a phone unless I was eighteen. When my baby's sick, I have to bring him out and take him to my mom's or to the corner phone booth in front of my house. It's foolish, because if he ever got hurt, not sick, but if he fell down, cut himself, I needed an ambulance, I'd have to take him with me to a phone booth to call for help. You know, it's ridiculous. But they won't give me one. I told them I was on social service; I could send in my Medicaid card, I could send in my I.D., and I sent them my Medicaid card; they just sent it back and they said it was their policy, they could not give it to me because of my age. I get help with money from social services, and besides I work. I get WIC too, and I get full assistance, Medicaid, food stamps, and cash grants, plus I work.

After I had my baby I wanted to move. My parents are separated. It was just my mom. I would still have been able to get assistance for my son, but I wanted to move out because I have a big family and my mom had a small house. My brothers and sisters would come over with their families, and there was so much noise and confusion; I would never have any time to think when I would come home from school. Everyone would be around my son because my mom used to baby-sit him when I first had him—until I got day care at school. And I didn't have time with him when he was little, then I would have homework, so I just moved out. Well, the day care at school depends on your attendance, your grades. You have to be in school and request day care. After you request it, you get put on a list, and if your name comes up and you have been in attendance and you don't cause problems and have a good attitude, they'll give you day care. If you're on social services, you can also get day care. Social services will provide, will pay for, day care elsewhere. They also pay for transportation to the day care. If you are not on social services, they usually make other arrangements if it's absolutely necessary if I can't find no one to take care of my child and I have to come to school. You can't miss school because you don't have day care. I think it's a fair policy. They shouldn't have day care if you're going to abuse it.

I don't find many problems with anything here; I mean, it's really a privilege, you know. You can still get your educational diploma, and if you can't accept it, you can leave and go back to high school. For one thing, they don't need day care in the high school; if they have it outside the school, it'd be a lot easier to go back to your home school; you have your friends, you can go to all the dances, you know. You're right there in a high school with boys and girls, where you can meet other people, have different teachers. But when you don't have day care, sometimes you're not allowed back at the school. When you don't have day care outside and you need it here, you have to stay here. You have to stay at the school [AECYM].

If I didn't have no other problems, just day care, I'd go back to my other high school, but here, they give you full attention, they show you child care, anything that you need to know about learning what to do, how to react to your child's behavior, how to potty train them, anything, they'll show you. The classes are small, so you get more attention. They give you more time, they're more patient and understanding if you have a baby; at the other school, they wouldn't have time for that. Sometimes it can be a little nerve-wracking; I mean, I was an accelerated student before I came to the alternative school. And they don't have that here, because of the limited [number of] teachers. So you get mixed in with average and basic students that take forever to [have] something [explained], and you have to wait. Sometimes it gets a little nerve-wracking, but other times, you think, well, it's a privilege. They give you day care; they're giving you an education; be patient.

The teachers here are excellent. They really take time. They don't just pass you if you're a nice student. Teachers that I have had at high school would pass students just to pass them. Or if they get all their homework assignments and even if they failed every test, they would pass. Teachers here make sure you know the information.

Another problem I have is going to the laundromat. It's just right across the street, but I have to carry our clothes and the baby down from the third floor across the street. I take him with me. He's a year and a half. It's hard because there's a busy street right there; I have to carry him and the clothes down the stairs and across the street. Then when I get in the laundromat, it's not too bad 'cause he'll just play. He sticks to me, really. He listens good, so when I call him, he'll come right to me. Then when I get done, I have to carry him and the clothes back across the street and back up the stairs.

Another good thing about the alternative school is the counselors here. They provide information. They would send you to a crisis center, help you find information in the phone books. They hand out pamphlets. Most of the time I have someone to talk to. My friends, my best friends, really support me. I have one friend who's a year older than me. She's easy to talk to. I'm used to solving everything myself. I don't really talk about my problems to anybody. I just talk to my best friend. We have about the same problems. She has a baby. She lives on her own.

Another good thing about the school is the fact I can work here. That's what I do right now. This is a job-training experience and office experience [which] I did last summer too. I did it as a summer job. I'll be working this summer too. I work in the office just a period out of the day, and during the summer, I work all day long. Eight hours. Last year, in typing class I had a high score, so Mrs. Pace asked me if I wanted to work in the office, for office experience. I went through the youth program. In the future I'm going to college. I've looked at working with computers, but I like working with people, too. So I don't know yet what I want to do. There's financial aid, and I can get on programs with social services, transportation, day care, books, and all this.

One thing I want to say, when I was pregnant, I was so young; I had to tell my mom, but I didn't want to tell her first 'cause I was so young, I knew she would be upset. I was only fifteen when I was pregnant, and I was sixteen when I had my son. I told my mom first, and then after that I told my brothers and my sisters. We went to the doctor. Then I registered for the school and then I applied for social services through Medicaid. I didn't talk to anybody about it; I just told myself I would do it on my own with or without [anyone's] support, I would make it; it was my happening. I wasn't going to give my child up. My brother's girlfriend came here; she had my nephew when she was fifteen. She helped me some. Social service also mentioned the alternative school when I applied there. My mom called and arranged an appointment with the counselor. Then we came down here, took a look around the school, and I came in September of 1989. It's hard being a teen parent, but each situation is different. I was in one situation. People have a lot: sometimes their parents are supportive, sometimes they throw them out of the house. I would like to tell counselors that I think teen parents should just be treated as adults. We have babies, we have responsibilities, and some of [the teen parents] are immature, and sometimes the counselors don't provide information; [the teen parents] should try to grow up and take on responsibilities; [the counselors] don't set them on the right track to know that they could handle it; they could make them want to stay at home, and some don't do that. Most people try to talk you into staying home. They want you to stay home with your parents, let you lean on your parents for a while, let your mother and your father help you raise your child. A lot of people try to talk you into doing that or [giving] your baby to your parents, while you continue to go to school. They mention other options, such as you raising your child and being a student, but they don't like to carry it out as much as they [press you] to stay home.

I wish people would ask me how I feel about being a teen mother. They always ask you how your parents feel, how the baby's father feels, how your friends feel toward you, how the school feels toward you, but they never really come right out and say, "How about your feelings to-

ward being a mother so young? Do you feel you are not going to be accepted by your friends? Do you feel you are going to be different from everyone else?" You know, no one ever asks you that question, how you really feel; they just ask everyone else how they feel. They don't put themselves there. I don't feel different. My friends all accepted me as being a mother. I came to this school; I still have friends at high school. It wasn't really different. I don't feel ashamed of it, but they never asked.

Jamie is but one student who attended the alternative school at the time of this study. In her words, one sees values, conflicts, gaps in the delivery system, and a lack of synchronization between Jamie's real life and the delivery system. These issues are reflected in the voices of other teens as well.

When I spoke with the teen mothers at the alternative school, they discussed a variety of topics. First, for the sake of clarity, the rest of the chapter presents their views about educational options of pregnant and parenting teens. Next, their needs are presented in their words and in four sections: basic needs, health needs, life skills, and "soft skills overall."

Educational Options

The AECYM operated two distinct programs: clients in the western region generally attended the in-school AECYM for parenting adolescents, and an outreach component of the program was developed to service the eastern rural end of the county. During 1989, 232 clients (appendix L) were enrolled in educational and vocational programs through the AECYM and 217 clients were served through the center's outreach program.

Clients had several options regarding school attendance:

1. Clients could remain in their regular school and attend regular classes.

2. Clients could attend the AECYM's alternative junior and senior high school education program (the model for this study.)

3. Pregnant and parenting students interested in vocational training could attend an alternative education program (including vocational classes) at the local Board of Coopera-

tive Educational Services, located in the eastern region of
the county.

4. Teen parents could choose to drop out of school.

5. Students who had dropped out of school could return to
the regular high school or alternative education programs.

6. Students with complicated medical problems could be tutored in their homes (see appendix I).[1]

During the months I spent at the center, I had an opportunity
to interview twenty-seven teen mothers and observe over fifty clients involved in these settings. Based on this information, as well as
the thirteen written responses to the student-developed questionnaire, at least seven factors influenced the decision of a teen parent
regarding school attendance: (a) location, (b) peer influence, (c) pa-
rental/familial influence, (d) personal motivation, (e) racism, (f)
court orders, and (g) outside pressure.

These factors were particularly important for teen parents in
the eastern, rural end of the county. Further, these seven factors
motivated the establishment of the alternative education program
in the eastern region of the county, according to counselors and administrators at the local Board of Cooperative Education Services
(BOCES). This program could be viewed as a competitor with the
AECYM, which is located in the western, urban region of the county.
Many of the rural clients were not in school or attended one of the
rural schools. There was a hesitation on the part of some rural clients to attend the "big city school with those types of girls" (client
comment). One counselor interpreted this to mean "black, druggies,
tough." The counselor and an administrator also reported the following comments made by students: "It's too far." "I'll spend too
much time on the bus." "How will I get there if I miss the bus?"
"My friends are here."

For these reasons, among others, the BOCES started its own
alternative education center for young mothers. The outreach counselors from the western AECYM did make regularly scheduled visits
to the BOCES program and did consider the students there to be
their clients. The BOCES program afforded the pregnant and
parenting teens of the county an additional educational option.

The existence of these two programs—as well as adult basic

training programs, which allowed parenting teens to return to school later in life—increased the chance that teen parents would complete a high school education.

Needs of Teen Parents

A data sheet for interviews with clients and their family support system was used, to focus the discussions around the needs of the clients (see appendix D). Originally fourteen categories were listed: food, clothing, shelter, physical health, mental health, education, vocational training, recreation, finances, transportation, child care, employment, religious affiliation, and other. During the course of the study, these categories began to fall into four general areas: basic needs, health needs, life skills, and "soft skills." Basic needs included food, clothes, and shelter. Mental and physical health were collapsed into a single area, health needs. Education, vocational training, finances, employment, transportation, and child care formed the area of concern called "life skills." Religious involvement and recreation emerged as a separate area called "soft skills," a term coined by the director of the AECYM to describe the quality-of-life needs of teen parents.

Basic Needs

The teen parents indicated that their basic needs (food, clothing, and shelter) were generally met satisfactorily. The teens listed the counselors at the AECYM as the primary sources of information for helping to fill a basic need. However, the teen parents also indicated that other parenting teens, family members, and friends provided information and support.

The existence of a client network in which service-delivery information was exchanged surfaced during this investigation. When asked how they knew about specific services, almost 90 percent indicated that a friend or relative had either received services themselves or knew of the service through another friend or relative. Through this second- and sometimes third-hand information system, clients were aware of at least some information about the system.

The outreach clients indicated in the written survey that family and friends shared equally in providing information and support.

Boyfriends were the third most often mentioned support and information source for the teen mother.

Most teen parents received food stamps, checks from the Women, Infants, and Children (WIC) supplemental food program, and assistance from their families including husbands and boyfriends. The clients indicated that without these subsidized food programs they would not be able to provide adequate food (especially infant formula) for their children. In the written survey, 92 percent of the outreach clients indicated that they received subsidized food checks through WIC, 76 percent received food stamps, 23 percent received assistance from their parents, 38 percent received assistance from their boyfriends, 7 percent received assistance from their husbands who worked, and 7 percent supported themselves by working. It is evident that the federally funded food programs sustained the teen parent. Any cuts in funding would have seriously affected nutrition for the teen mothers and their children.

The teen parents attending school generally indicated that they had adequate clothing. If they did not, 61 percent of the clients surveyed knew where to find assistance if they needed clothing for themselves or their children. In the written survey, 62 percent of the outreach clients stated they needed clothing for themselves and 69 percent needed clothing for their children. However, 61 percent knew where to find assistance. They listed places such as Goodwill, Salvation Army, and Clothes Closets, a local retail store. What was meant by "need clothing"? Since some clients gave "retail outlet stores" as a response, their "need" may actually have been for trendy, stylish clothes reflective of any teenager's desire for contemporary clothes.

This poses an interesting question for policymakers and service providers. When is a need a need and not just a want? Should wants be funded? In this case, whether the question was viewed as a need or a want, 88 percent of those who "needed" clothing knew where to go for assistance. In that sense, their need could be adequately satisfied.[2] However, 12 percent (this includes both in-school and outreach clients) did not know where to secure services. Therefore, some teen parents were not receiving information on available services.

The availability of laundry facilities was another issue related to

clothing. In this case, the issue was viewed as a child care problem
rather than a laundry problem.[3] One young mother had to leave
her child upstairs unattended while she carried each load of laundry
down the stairs and to the laundromat across the street. She would
then leave the clothes unattended at the laundromat and go back
and get her child. She realized that leaving a child unattended not
only was dangerous but also could result in a child-neglect case
against her. However, she couldn't figure out a better system. Therefore, she viewed this as a child care problem. The laundry problem
was even more complicated if transportation was required. If a teen
mother could drive, did she have access to a car, enough gas, or
money for gas? If she did not drive, who would take her? Was a taxi
available?

With the assistance of the counselors at the AECYM, most teen
mothers were able to meet their laundry needs. Therefore, in general the clothing and laundry needs of the parenting teens were adequately met with assistance. When clients needed additional assistance, they knew where to go.[4]

This is an example of how the developmental level of the clients
affected their ability to access services. The services were available
during the time of the study, but the clients needed someone to help
them sort through the problem, see the alternatives, and work through
the issues.

In most cases clients felt their shelter was adequate (see appendix J for the demographics of their living arrangements). In some
cases, however, clients were forced at the age of sixteen to move into
their own apartments in order to be eligible for welfare even though
they would have preferred to remain with a parent or guardian. The
policy of using the entire household budget to determine eligibility
for financial assistance is particularly difficult for young couples who
want to stay together. A young twenty-three-year-old husband of a
twenty-one-year-old wife with three children stated:

They [social services] encourage—she could have had everything on a
silver platter if she divorced me. They encourage the breakup of mar-
riages. She was told, "We can only help you so much with the children,
but if you would separate we could help you more."

At least three groups of teen parents were poorly served by the system. The first were the fifteen-year-old or younger teen mothers who were forced to stay in a seriously (yet nonprovable) abusive family situation in order to get financial assistance. The second were the sixteen-year olds who would have liked to stay with their families but were forced to move in order to receive financial support for themselves and their children. The third group was composed of young low-income couples who, with a little assistance, could make great strides. As a twenty-one-year-old wife who was pregnant as a young teen stated: "It doesn't always have to be in the form of food stamps or money—just counseling . . . help with budgeting or planning. Something to help you see what you're doing wrong that makes you need welfare." The majority of the cases reviewed indicated that the system was adequate in providing financial support for housing to pregnant and parenting teens, thanks to the assistance of counselors and social workers.

Clients said they received financial assistance for their housing from (a) welfare, (b) rent subsidies, (c) social services, (d) parents, or (e) boyfriends. In one case, the young mother lived in an apartment building owned by her parents and her boyfriend paid the rent. None of the clients interviewed or surveyed were homeless. One client was living in a domestic-violence shelter.

Although housing arrangements were adequate, the students said if they were single parents and heads of household at age seventeen or younger, they had difficulty getting utility services. Companies providing utilities such as telephone services would not provide them to anyone under the age of eighteen even if that person could provide evidence of income. This could prove particularly difficult for a teen mother who needed to make an emergency phone call because of a sick child. Should she take her sick child out on a cold winter night in order to call a doctor from the nearest pay phone, or should she leave her child unattended in the apartment while she phones the doctor's office? In either case she could be viewed as a negligent mother. Although there were other alternatives, such as having a phone arrangement with a neighbor, these contingency plans required organizational, planning and critical-thinking skills that may not yet have been acquired by a teen parent.

This is one example of how teen parents are "pinched" by conflicting regulations. They are able to live as single parents and heads of households when they are sixteen. In some cases, they are encouraged to do so by service providers as well as their own family members, so they can take care of their child financially. Yet, they cannot get phone service until they are eighteen. So for two years, when a teen parent is most vulnerable with an infant and in most need of support, she is without a phone and often without the skills necessary to plan for emergencies.

Based on interviews or written surveys with over fifty teen parents, it appears that their basic needs of food, clothing, and shelter were being adequately met through the service-delivery system studied. It is important to note that their needs were being met *through the service-delivery system*, that is, with the assistance of the direct-service providers who worked with the clients to think through their unmet needs, reviewed their resources and options, and provided concrete services when needed. However, any cuts in services would have drastically reduced this adequacy. Therefore, funding of the federal food subsidies must continue at least at current levels. Dissemination of information regarding existing clothing services should be increased. When planning living arrangements, the Department of Social Services needs to develop programs that take into account the individual needs of each teen parent. At the program administration level, an effort should be made to work with utility companies when conflicting policies prevent clients from receiving adequate services.

Health Needs

The health needs of parenting teens was the second topic addressed in the interviews and surveys of teen parents. The clients eagerly discussed their physical health needs and those of their children, but they seemed reluctant to discuss mental health needs.

In preparing the written survey, the seniors of the AECYM civics class posed the following questions as a reflection of mental services: "Do you have someone to talk to in a stressful situation?" and "If a friend or member of your family needed mental help, would you know where to go for help?" The second question was specifically designed by the seniors to eliminate any negative stereotyping that might cause clients to be uncomfortable. The seniors felt that the clients would respond more readily if the question focused on someone other than themselves.

It can be argued that these two questions did not adequately address the mental health concerns of pregnant and parenting teens. However, these questions were prepared by teen parents, and from their perspective these questions did reflect their concerns.

From the point of view of the clients, the mental health services were adequate. The clients stated that they knew where to go or whom to contact if they or their friends needed special mental health services to deal with drug abuse or suicide or needed general counseling.[5] In the written survey, 92 percent of the outreach clients indicated that they had someone to talk to in a stressful situation, while 82 percent indicated that they knew where to go for help if they, a family member, or a friend needed to talk. Therefore, 8 percent of the respondents did not have anyone to talk to and 18 percent did not know where to go for assistance. However, none of the respondents asked for information in the space provided on the survey. Based on the survey and the high percentage of clients who had someone to talk to or knew where to secure information, there was no articulated need for additional mental health services from the clients' perspectives.

Regarding their physical needs, clients were generally very satisfied with their prenatal, obstetric, and postnatal care. They indicated that the medical staff at the local medical clinic were generally supportive. A part-time social worker acted as a liaison between the clients and the medical staff by interpreting medical and pharmaceutical information for the clients and by updating the medical staff on any client circumstance that might impinge on the client's ability to follow medical directions. Although counselors at the AECYM also provided this service, some of the social workers whom I interviewed reported that the clients had mentioned that more social workers at the medical center would be beneficial.

Teen parents could also easily obtain pediatric care for their children. At the alternative school, the director of the day care component—as a registered nurse—conducted daily screening of the children in attendance, notified the school nurse of any illness, and made appropriate referrals for medical care. Even those teen parents who had alternative day care arrangements had access to pediatricians in the area.

A difficulty did arise, however, when a teen parent had a medical problem not related to the pregnancy. Two responses to the health care questions on the survey for outreach clients were: "I need a family physician myself. Children have a physician—I don't, except for an obstetrician" and "Yes, I have a physician for being pregnant, for my kids, but when I'm not pregnant, I don't have a physician." Most of the parenting teens interviewed did not have access to the services of a general practitioner for their own health care, and there were a variety of reasons for this: (*a*) for some teen mothers preventive/general health care was not seen as important now that they were no longer pregnant; (*b*) issues of birth control could be dealt with through family planning agencies, so that a private physician wasn't necessary; (*c*) the clients lacked the financial resources; and (*d*) younger teens were confused as to the type of physician that would be most appropriate for them (pediatrician, general practitioner, adolescent specialist, or family practitioner). Therefore, the clients generally used the local hospital emergency room for their own health needs other than pregnancy.

From the teens' perspective, their pregnancy-related health needs were adequately met by the existing service-delivery system, but they were in need of a personal physician. A possible way to address this issue might be the establishment of a formal agreement between the AECYM and local family physicians to provide educational programs, preventive-medicine programs, or both. Since a physician and other medical personnel are on the center's board of directors, initial linkages are already in place.

Life Skills

Job training, education, and "real world" skills (such as budgeting, parenting, and communication) are often lumped into the category of life skills. In other words, *life skills* refer to those competencies necessary for one to function as a productive member of society once basic needs are met. The process of becoming productive involves a variety of skills including, but not limited to, such activities as setting goals, personal hygiene and grooming, and job training.

Education, vocational training, employment, finances, transportation, and child care issues were intertwined in the life skills of the parenting teens. Transportation was the major barrier to receiving basic services. Compounding the issue of transportation was the fact that the public transportation system was undergoing financial difficulties and was shut down during part of the research period.

The issue of transportation was reiterated by almost every client interviewed. The written survey revealed that none of the outreach clients in rural areas owned a car. Figure 5.1 shows the frequency with which each means of transportation was used.

The lack of transportation was seen as a major barrier to achieving self-sufficiency. Transportation, day care, and employment/training were viewed as intertwined and often as a hopeless situation. Child care and transportation were provided while a client was in school. Once a client was out of school and ready to enter the job market, she still needed day care and transportation to go for job interviews. Once she secured a job, these three factors become even more interdependent. If a child was sick and could not go to the day care center, who would take care of her child if the mother went to work? What happened if the public transportation system was down or she had no money for gas, or what happened if the car broke down? These problems are also faced by many single working mothers and dual-career families of today. However, teen parents sometimes did not have the experience or resourcefulness to deal with

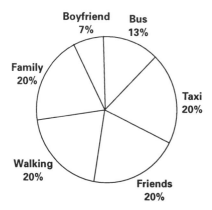

Figure 5.1. Frequency of Means of Transportation

such situations. Several of the teen parents interviewed stated that they were too overwhelmed by the logistics of the situation to even try to look for a job.

Through the counseling component of the AECYM and its referral network, a system was in place during this research project to support clients during their high school years. Teens who had dropped out of school could return for job training and vocational education through various community programs. However, once a client graduated or finished a training program, little if any follow-up was available to her.

This situation created a pool of clients who might work for a short time and then find that they were unable to cope with the various stresses of single parenthood, employment, and family problems. As long as a teen mother was in the service-delivery system centered around the alternative school, she had ongoing and varied support. However, once a teen parent moved into her early twenties, she might no longer qualify for services and was often isolated and without support. Strides toward self-sufficiency made during the previous years of schooling or training might be reversed or undermined. While discussing this balance of transportation, day care, and employment, one teen parent stated: "I found out by looking at the system—it looks like sometimes the system trains you, makes you want to stay on it [welfare]." Welfare provided assistance with transportation and job training but "not really enough to get out of the system, just enough to keep you in."

This example points out a shortcoming of the service-delivery system with regard to life skills. As the term *life skills* implies, services are needed to help disadvantaged teen parents cope with life, not just the one or two years they are in school. By providing only short-term support, the system sometimes fails to provide enough support to help clients "out of the system." Teen parents need ongoing support, especially during periods of transition, for example, after high school graduation and before securing a job, or during second pregnancies in the late teens or early twenties.

It was evident that from the client's perspective the present service-delivery system was making some strides in the areas of child care, education, and transportation. However, the system fell short at crucial transitional periods and may foster entrenchment in the system.

Soft Skills

The term *soft skills* describes the tools needed to develop the attitudes and behaviors characteristic of a "caring" pregnant or parenting teen. Through the use of these skills, pregnant and parenting teens begin to demonstrate a respect for themselves, their children, their family and friends, their significant others, and people in general. The term summarizes characteristics generally associated with the self-sufficiency that enables a person to become a contributing member of society. Although these skills could be discussed as mental health issues, the term *mental health* often refers to formal health care through counseling, hospitalization, or some other type of professional care. Soft skills are part of everyday life and are generally not part of the professional health care system.

Throughout the research process, most program administrators and direct-service providers described a successful teen parent as one who could care for herself and her child. This definition included the expectation that parenting teens could support themselves and their children financially. A more elusive quality of the definition concerns how the client measures up to some standard of emotional or psychological caring, which is understood by each service provider and program administrator in his or her own way. This caring is characterized by such attitudes as thoughtfulness, empathy, and giving.

Thoughtfulness commonly means to think of others, to consider their feelings, but it also means being absorbed in thought and, by extension, the ability to reflect on, to think about, to meditate on, and to center oneself. These skills bridge the gap between cognition and intuition. Thoughtfulness is the ability to find meaning in the present situation. Here is an example that describes how one young mother found meaning in her life.

Ellen, a mother at the age of fifteen, attended the alternative school during 1971, its second year of operation. At the time of the interview (1990), she was employed as an accountant at one of the largest industries in the community and was on the executive board of the alternative school. Ellen married six years before at the age of 29, when her son was 13, and now had two other young children with her husband. During the interview, Ellen discussed a religious experience to which she attributed her success and from which she derived a sense of meaning.

For me it was a very positive religious experience that turned my life around. May I add that I accepted Christ when my son was six months old. I can really attest to that. That's what really turned my life around. That attitude of mine changed me as well. So what if this guy dumps me? I'm still somebody—God loves me and I can go forward. Right during that time I was probably very depressed and things were not going my way. I remember asking, "Who do you turn to?" My mom had her problems, I was an only child, I had no extended family. I turned to the Lord and I asked him to come into my life and to help me . . . and something happened inwardly. . . . I know it did.

Shortly after this experience, Ellen's boyfriend married someone else. She then went on to discuss the feelings of self-worth that developed as a result of this experience.

Nothing can be more deflating to someone's esteem than having someone who you've given yourself to physically as well as emotionally [leave you], becoming pregnant, and then being left alone. That will deflate your esteem . . . it's like a divorce. . . . So esteem is important: knowing that you are worth something and then that the sense of pride can only roll over in the child, knowing that I'm somebody worth more than you're making me feel like [referring to her boyfriend].

Through this religious experience Ellen developed a "real relationship" (her term) with a higher power and, in so doing, felt worthwhile. It is this sense of self-worth and pride that Ellen sought to instill in other teen parents. As a member of the alternative school advisory board, Ellen said: "[I would like] to see these young girls become major contributors in society, not deficits but [people] that can stand on their own two feet and take care of themselves and their child, not wait on welfare or society to take care of them." She suggested that teen mothers could seek support in their quest to become productive members of society through the alternative school, which became her "pseudo family," and through their churches, which played an important role in the community.

The interior relationship Ellen described was described by Jung (cited in Progoff 1973) as the process of individuation through which an individual comes to "know the self," the interior or "driving" force. Ellen's ability to reflect on the events that led her to discover "meaning" in her situation is an example of the thoughtfulness that leads to caring for oneself and others. As Ellen said, "Knowing that you are worth something and then that the sense of pride can only roll over in the child."[6]

An example of the empathy associated with soft skills was demonstrated by the husband of a former AECYM client. He supported his wife during her teen years. When asked about the type of service he needed in order to support his twenty-one-year-old wife and mother of three children now, this twenty-three-year-old man responded: "Counseling, to get some idea of what she was going through. I had no idea of what she was going through during the second pregnancy; during the third I had some idea." (His wife had one child with another partner prior to their marriage.) Every male interviewed wanted help in understanding what the teen mother was feeling and going through during and after her pregnancy.

Empathy was also exhibited by several of the seniors at the alternative school when they discussed the difficulties faced by the younger teen mothers who attended the school. Their comments included the following:

- "I had it easier; I got pregnant when I was a senior."
- "I don't know how they cope."
- "How will they stay in school for four years?"
- "You've got to have patience—they don't."
- "I had a lot of support—a lot of girls don't have support."
- "You just put yourself in their shoes to help them."

The seniors' comments revealed the beginnings of "being in another's shoes," which is associated with empathy. These examples of empathy were particularly important to the director as she discussed soft skills.

A third characteristic of soft skills is "giving," that is, thinking and acting for another's growth and well-being. The director of the school—as well as many board members, students, and service providers—felt that the goal of the various components of the program was to help clients become contributing members of the community and thereby give back to the community.

This attitude of giving was particularly evident in the social studies class at the school, where students were encouraged to write letters to the editor of the local newspaper, their congressional representatives, and national and local politicians. Through these activities, the teen parent could take an active role in learning citizenship and participating in the democratic process. It was in this civics class that students developed the written survey to outreach clients.

The program director forcefully communicated to me her desire to instill in the students a sense of control in their own lives and not to have them viewed (or to view themselves) as helpless victims. The civic activities of the social studies class were viewed by the staff of the school as an opportunity for the students to provide input into programs that had a direct impact on their lives.

These soft skills—related to communication, relationships, and the quality of life—are often difficult to teach and reflect what has been sometimes labeled as the "milieu," the attitudinal environment, the way we do things around here, or the culture of an organization (Deal and Kennedy 1982). Culture may be transmitted through (*a*) role modeling, (*b*) participation in community events, and (*c*) familiarity with the myths and stories of the culture. In the case of the alternative school, role modeling is evident in the daily activities of the staff. One teacher worked with the seniors to produce a video yearbook. His activity was cited by students as one example of how the staff "cares for" them at the AECYM. In addition, I worked with the senior civics class community involvement project to develop the written survey mentioned previously. Throughout this process the students were articulate in presenting their concerns about teen parenting and eager to help other teen parents.

Students understood the ethic of care that was central to the AECYM organizational philosophy. The young women were able to articulate how service delivery personnel went beyond the call of duty in helping them. Their stories about the kindnesses of the service providers served to support the quality-of-life notion that the director of the AECYM intended to foster among the students.

Soft skills deal with the quality of life, one aspect of which are recreational activities and leisure time pursuits. The parenting teens and young couples interviewed by me indicated that they had little time, money, or opportunity for recreation. They described the difficulties in attempting to get a dependable babysitter or finding a place where the mother and child could recreate together. Students also suggested the possibility of having drop-in day care, which would provide single mothers without support a respite during school vacations.

One student described her concern about an upcoming school vacation. This student normally brought her child with her to the AECYM's day care. The only time that this mother was away from her child was during the school day. She had virtually no support system from her family, and she lived alone with her child. During vacation time this seventeen-year-old teen mother would virtually spend two weeks in the constant company of her child.

Exposure to the arts was one way through which the students at the alternative school could transcend their present situation and begin to develop soft skills. For example, the students at the AECYM had an opportunity to see Shakespeare's *Macbeth* presented in a bomb shelter.

The quality-of-life issue is involvement with spiritual pursuits. The relationship of the pregnant and parenting teens with organized religion was briefly investigated during the interviews, but only Ellen (mentioned above) discussed it in depth. Those teen parents who felt a need to participate in a religious organization did so. If they were rejected by their congregation, they left that church and attended a church that was more accepting of their situation. One client reported that the religious group to which she belonged provided her with some clothing and that "they were nice to me." Overall, organized religion was not viewed by the teen parents as either overly supportive or problematic.[7]

Based on these discussions, it is evident that the development of programs in the area of soft skills has only slowly been emerging. Conditions exist for understanding the quality of life through religious organizations, caring professionals, recreational opportunities, and the pursuit of fine arts. However, no clear plan for developing soft skills exists in the service-delivery system, and in some cases, a realization of the importance of soft skills is lacking.

Pregnant Teens Fifteen Years of Age or Younger

A special focus was placed on the problems faced by teen mothers under the age of fifteen. Although there were definite legal problems faced by this younger group of teens, most of the people interviewed (including teen parents, direct-service providers, and family support members), felt that age was not an important factor in how successful a teen mother was in completing school. Most of the interviewees believed that family support and family background were the key to whether a young mother under the age of fifteen completed school. Even clients who gave birth at that early age and were now seventeen or older felt strongly that their family support network was the sustaining factor in their successful attendance at school.

Paula, a seventeen-year-old who worked with me on the client outreach survey and who had her child at age fifteen, remarked, "My mother helped me a lot. Some girls don't have anybody. Some seventeen-year-olds don't have anybody. It's hard when there's no one to help you no matter how old you are."

Several direct-service providers, particularly those involved with public assistance programs, pointed out the difficulties for teen parents under the age of fifteen who did not have parental support. Clients under the age of sixteen were considered part of the parental household when eligibility for public assistance was determined. Therefore, if a young parent was in a borderline abusive situation, sometimes little could be done to provide her with public assistance in establishing her own household or with temporary housing either in foster care or a group home.[8] Once the teen mother was sixteen, arrangements could be made to establish her as the head of her own household. As one family member reported:

She [parenting teen] has always been a private person. She's wanted to be on her own. When she lived with me, we didn't always see eye to eye. We do get along better now that she has her own place. She'll bring the baby over. I'll call and tell her she has mail. But working with Social

Services was hard; there was always some excuse not to get an apartment. It was very discouraging.

This policy of installing teen mothers as the head of a household was viewed ambivalently by some service providers, family members, and clients. Although it was generally felt that young teen mothers should remain at home and that they needed the support of their families, situations arose in which the teen mother was "trapped" in an extremely dysfunctional family situation. Other interviewees discussed the opposite situation, in which teen mothers who wanted to remain with their families were forced to move into their own apartment when they turned sixteen in order to receive financial assistance from the Department of Social Services.

This dilemma was vividly brought to the researcher's attention during a group interview with the ninth-grade students of the AECYM. The following lively discussion illustrates their unique housing situations:

Student 1:	I tried to move out when I was fifteen, but I couldn't. They [Department of Social Services (DSS)] kept telling me I couldn't.
Student 2:	They told me I had to.
Researcher:	How old were you?
Student 2:	Sixteen.
Student 3:	My mom's a real help. I wanted to stay, but I didn't want to be a burden to my mom. I couldn't get anything because my mom works at the chemical plant. If me and the baby moved out, DSS would help.
Student 4:	I like being on my own. I couldn't wait to get out.
Student 4 to Student 1:	Where do you live now?
Student 1:	With my boyfriend.

Parenting teens around the age of fifteen appear to be caught in borderline policy dilemmas. Because of the developmental level and unique family background of each client, general policy regulations often mitigated against "best service" for a particular client, as the foregoing example demonstrates. One way in which the state's Department of Social Service workers made the policy more "client friendly" was through implementation of a Special Services act. Through this act client caseloads were reduced, a single case manager worked with the entire family, and caseworkers could cut through "red tape" through special in-house procedures. Teen parents viewed the Special Services Act program very positively. When clients were asked, "If a friend told you she was pregnant, where would you tell her to go for help?" the second-largest number of responses after the AECYM was a Special Services Act caseworker.

In summary, parenting teens fifteen years of age or younger are in a transitional place legally: moving from the status of child to legal emancipation as a head of household at sixteen. This period of transition is difficult and may be compared "to the edges of any landscape . . . to the earth's twilight place . . . where what is critical straddles a border between being what it is and becoming something else" (Lopez 1987, 110). These twilight places are difficult to traverse. It is only with direct, constant, and consistent support that a young teen can successfully make the transition from child to parent.

Aside from legal and housing concerns, parenting teens fifteen years old or younger have the same needs (housing, clothing, food, etc.) as other teen parents. Providing services to this age group is difficult because of their developmental level. Given that service providers meet each client "where they are" developmentally, socially, and physically, as well as the fact that each client has unique needs, it is the responsibility of the service provider to determine how to assist the clients in meeting their needs.

Two issues in regard to the pregnancies of young women under the age of fifteen that have received little attention in the past but are emerging as important issues are incest and the age of the male partner (Boyer 1995; Males 1995). Although these issues are extremely sensitive, they were not explored in this study.

Summary

Through my interviews with teen parents, it becomes evident that in the service-delivery system studied:

- A wide range of educational opportunities existed for parenting teens.
- Parenting teens fifteen years of age or under had the same set of needs (food, clothing, shelter, day care, etc.) as other parenting teens but were caught in transitional situations in which governmental regulations conflicted, and they often did not have the problem-solving skills required for parenting. In addition, further research into the effects of the age of their male partner and incestuous relationships needs to be conducted.
- The basic needs of food, clothing, and shelter were adequately being met at present levels for most clients through the service-delivery system and the service provider, who assisted in solving problems.
- Clients generally lacked a personal physician for medical problems other than pregnancy.
- The development of life skills was a complex intertwining of education, job training, employment, day care, and transportation. The present service-delivery system addressed these issues for in-school parenting teens. The system fell short in serving parents in their late teens and early twenties or when they left school.
- The issue of quality of life[9] through the development of soft skills is a new frontier to be explored and includes such concrete activities as recreational opportunities, religious affiliation, and civic participation.

Based on the input of the parenting teens, gaps in services did not exist at the basic needs level during this study, but large gaps in services did exist at the soft skills level. There was therefore a gradual widening of the gap in services from basic needs to soft skills. Those clients who attended the AECYM related fewer problems with service delivery than did outreach clients because services such as day care and counseling were available on site during school hours. This link between services and educational opportunities was viewed as central to "making it as a teen parent," as one client commented.

Notes

1. The home tutoring forms provided in appendix I were used at an alternative education setting that was not part of this study. However, they are included here as a resource for practitioners. I have been asked to provide this information to practitioners who are initiating tutoring programs for pregnant and parenting teens, and I am aware of four single-site alternative education programs that were started as tutoring programs.

2. As stated in the section of chapter 2 titled "Assumptions and Limitations," knowing where to go for services is only one indication that the client's needs are being met.

3. No client introduced the issue of laundry by herself; I raised the question of the availability of laundry facilities. In most cases, clients had laundry facilities in their apartment complexes or homes. Difficulties arose when clients lived alone and had to go to the laundromat.

4. Knowing where to go for services is only the prelude to obtaining them.

5. The clients were not asked directly about costs, child care concerns, or transportation issues directly related to mental health services.

6. Issues related to the meaning teen parents place on their parenting experiences have rarely been explored by researchers. Ellen's comments are provocative and are offered here in an attempt to stimulate dialogue.

7. Initially the researcher limited the interview to a discussion of the support for parenting teens from organized religious groups. It was only through the interview with Ellen that the need for an understanding of the spiritual, reflective life of the pregnant and parenting teen became evident. This is one area of research that has been rarely explored at present.

8. See Marecek (1995) for more information on helping teens cope with abusive relationships.

9. Issues of caring are emerging in various pieces of literature on school administration (Beck 1994) and other professions (Noddings 1984, 1988, 1989, 1992, 1995).

Chapter Six
The Voice of Support People

The teen mothers revealed that they received various types of support from family members, their classmates at the AECYM or in the group outreach program, and various staff members of the AECYM. This support included but was not limited to transportation, child care, and financial and emotional assistance. The type of support did not appear to be as important as the "quality" of support. Phrases such as "I can trust her" and "She's a big help" punctuated the teen mothers' remarks when the topic of support was discussed.

Based on the interviews with the teen mothers, thirteen support people not including the direct-service providers were identified and interviewed: (a) five peers, (b) three mothers of teen mothers, (c) two boyfriends, (d) a father of a teen mother, (e) a husband of a teen mother, and (f) a grandmother. The teen mothers mentioned peers as support people generally in cases where the teen mother lived alone with her child. In nearly all the other cases, the teen mother lived with the person who provided support.

The teen mothers indicated that peers provided overall emotional support: "She was always there for me. I'd listen to her problems. She'd listen to my problems, and when I was real depressed about what I was going to do about my baby, she'd tell me to do what makes me happy."

Among the peer group self-help support groups evolved, and through them child care, transportation, and shopping services were exchanged among the teen mothers. Recreation was defined by the teen mothers as an opportunity to shop or visit with each other and their children. Since the members of these peer support groups experienced similar problems and needs, any help provided to one teen mother had a residual impact on the others through their increased knowledge of where and how to procure services.

The support people who lived with the teen mothers reported that their relationship with the teen mothers was the most important consideration. Nearly all of these support people mentioned the need for help in understanding the teen mother. For example, the parents of a teen mother who were interviewed in their home stated that the service providers "need to form some groups to help make it easier to understand what their children are going through because a majority of parents have no idea how scared they [the teen parents] are." Although "support" can have a different meaning for different people, all the parents of the teen mothers indicated a need for some type of support group for themselves.[1]

The teen fathers also indicated that they needed help in their relationships with the teen mothers. The husband mentioned in chapter 5 of a woman who was pregnant as a teen and now had three children talked about the type of counseling services he needed:

Counseling to get some idea of what she [teen mother] was going through. I had no idea of what she was going through during the second one. During the third, I had some idea. Also I could have used classes on parenting, just how to change diapers . . . help to understand what the children are going through, the ages that they're going through, child development. Classes for mothers and fathers. Sometimes I make mistakes with my kids; I think they're older than what they are; I expect them to do a lot more, what I tell them; I expected my four-year-old and two-year-old to do it. . . . How to punish without hurting.

This quote exemplifies how the father had concern for his family and had a need to be of support but yet how he himself was in need.

Teen fathers are a unique group of support people because of their intimate relationship with the teen mother. They not only provide support but are in need of support themselves. Insight into the life of a teen father was provided by Bob.

Bob, a father at the age of seventeen and now the director of the local boys club, discussed the importance of a role model in the life of teen fathers. He said that he was fortunate to have his own father as a role model.

I was a teen father, so I knew the routine. I know what they go through because I've been there myself, so I said that I was fortunate enough— I'll use the word "blessed" also—to have made it this far.

So I said that if I ever made it, it was my obligation to help others.

Thank God I had a father who I just sort of role modeled myself after. If the young man hasn't had a father, where does he get it? . . . At some point you have to have an experience, . . . a relationship that jars you . . . where you can build a relationship with a male, a role model. . . . Now they begin to see, to form themselves after the other male.

Bob suggested that the emptiness experienced by many teen fathers because of their own lack of a father could be alleviated by the experience of a positive relationship with another father figure, either a teacher in school or a coach or counselor at the boys club. He stressed the importance of personal contact and spent time in the community interacting informally with the young men who come to the boys club.

Bob had an open-door policy. Any child or young member of the boys club could come into his office at any time. Bob had worked there for over seventeen years and had a personal relationship with them. In this way, he hoped to provide an example of a caring father and to emphasize the importance of the teen father in the life of the teen father's child. He said:

The greatest impact you can have for your child is to be visible and to love that child regardless of the relationship between you and the young lady—whether you make it or not, because statistics say you're not going to make it. But even if you forget about statistics, still in some way keep a relationship with that mother and with that child. It's difficult for someone to understand.

Teen fathers are not alone in their role of providing support to the teen mother yet needing support themselves. Teen mothers indicated that they received tremendous emotional support from their children. When asked on the written survey to state their greatest joy, all the outreach clients responded that their children were their greatest joy. One client responded that her child was also her greatest frustration, and given the dynamics of parenting, this response was perhaps the most realistic. The joy and frustration of caring for a child is evident in the day care center at the AECYM. On any given day, I would observe some teen moms holding their children, focusing their attention directly on them, and enjoying lunchtime with them. Other mothers placed the food down in front of their child and walked away without talking, while still others commenced the daily "food battle."

The teen mother's relationship with her child typifies her relationships with her other support people. The ebb and flow of giving support yet desperately needing support was a thread in my interviews with support people. Among the suggestions given for helping the support people were parenting classes, support groups, counseling, and financial assistance. The support people indicated that they had a stake in the service-delivery system because it helped them care for and support the teen mother. The system falls short, however, in providing support for the support person.

Summary

Creative ways for supporting the "significant others" in the teen parents' lives need to be encouraged. Self-help groups for the parents of teen parents, counseling for the support persons, and parenting classes for males were some of the suggestions proposed by the family support members interviewed.

Note

1.   Jeanne Warren Lindsay (1995) explores the relationship between teen parents, their parents, and their children in her book *School-Age Parents: The Challenge of Three-Generation Living.*

Chapter Seven
The Voice of Direct-Service Providers

"When I first started, I thought, 'Oh, I'm going to get in here and I'm going to do everything right.' You know I'm going to make it right for these girls." This comment was echoed by several service providers. Most of the twenty-four service providers interviewed were motivated to help the teen parents, to somehow make a difference in their lives. Then reality strikes. The service provider just quoted went on to say, "Then that fell through. You realize that they are teenage mothers. . . . They can go to school and they can get a job, but still as a young mother they have lost that part of their youth and they will never get it back. It is very sad." Another service provider stated: "In other ways, too, it's frustrating; but to know that you've worked really hard with a client and you finally achieve something—it's the best feeling in the world." A third service provider described a successful client intervention:

I think you have to go from where the clients are at and see what they want to do and see where they want to go, unless that is detrimental . . . helping them see things as realistically as they can and even if you only take one step with them, that is still success. Even if a kid comes in and she is pregnant and she hasn't seen a doctor, if you get her into a doctor and you never see her again, at least she is going to the doctor. At least she is doing something.

The twenty-four direct-service providers were interviewed either individually or in focus groups. These groups—made up of teachers, nurses, health-related social workers, outreach counselors, nutrition counselors, parent aides, school counselors, and social workers—interacted directly with clients on a daily basis. They were the initial contacts between the client and the service-delivery system. During the interviews, these service providers demonstrated a concern and empathy for their clients and discussed their working conditions, organizational issues, professional preparation, and the importance of interagency collaboration.

Concern and Empathy for Clients

Depending on their profession, service providers used different words to refer to a teen parent. Teachers referred to them as "students," nurses and health professionals referred to them as "patients," and social workers called the teen parent a "client." Regardless of the term used to describe the teen mother, all of the service providers stated that their involvement in the service-delivery system and their choice of profession came from a desire to be of service and to help their clients. A successful client was generally seen as a teen mother who had the ability to make informed decisions and then carry them out. Most service providers saw themselves as providers of information who assisted clients in making appropriate decisions based on this information.

A social worker at a local clinic stated:

My role here, in terms of the physician, is to keep them up to date on the clients and, in this case, the teen mother and teen parents—progress in a social situation, to keep the communication channels open. [It's] real important for me that when the girl has a doctor, especially during her pregnancy, she has the communication of the doctor. She feels comfortable, she feels free to ask any question, and sometimes I kind of run interference between them just to make sure that she has the right information because a lot of times (I know even myself if I go to the doctors it's kind of scary), they are not asking the questions or they are not hearing the information correctly, and that's . . . where I come in. I kind of work in between them. So I could sit with the doctors. I try to help them, make them aware of the patients' needs. That's real important.

I think I would describe [a successful client] as probably a teen that comes and is willing to look at her options in terms of pregnancy, . . . is able to make some choices. Maybe someone that is receptive to getting linked up with the alternative school [and] is following through with

*me in terms of patient education, is keeping [her] doctor's appointments.
I follow them along with pregnancy to see how they are doing. [Someone
who] is receptive to family planning and who seems to be successful in
terms of the program that we do here. I guess that would be a successful
intervention in terms of the teen, knowing that they are continuing their
education. They are getting the right prenatal care, they are becoming
much more educated in terms of their bodies, in terms of once they have
their children. The medical needs of their children, you know, the normal things associated with the child's growth and development.*

Although these characteristics may be the desired outcome of a
successful intervention, the reality that service providers encounter
on a daily basis is often far from their expectations and hopes for
their clients. The service providers interviewed were concerned with
their clients' basic needs, health needs, life skills, and what has already been referred to as "soft skills." Although many of the clients
interviewed indicated that their basic needs were being met, the service providers were far more concerned with those needs. This may
be due to the fact that when the clients were in need of food, clothing, or shelter, they contacted their social worker or direct-service
provider. It was then the service provider's task to help the client
meet those needs.

Little consensus existed among the service providers as to
which basic need was not currently being met by the existing
service-delivery system. The following comments exemplify this
diversity:

- *Service Provider 1:* "I would say food [is the most important need] because shelter is seen as a necessity so they can
get that from the housing authority, the department of social services. They will always find a way to sleep in
someone's spare room, but more often than not I get calls
from the girls who have run out of formula, they've run out
of baby food, they've run out of this or that."
- *Service Provider 2:* "If somebody comes here and they don't
have food or clothing, the reason is because they have no
income."

Since these service providers were speaking from their own experiences, the diversity in identifying client need reflects the organizational and bureaucratic limitations that were particular to each provider's perspective. The providers did agree that isolation caused by lack of transportation was a barrier to existing services.

I think the girls who are isolated are more frustrated. . . . Most of the girls in our group are living in the city. . . . So they can walk around and get around town, but sometimes that is their only time to get with other people, too. Now the girls in our outreach rural program, in the western area, they don't even get a chance to do that. I mean physically and time-wise, we can't get them and bring them in. There is no way we can pick them all up and bring them to the city for our group meetings. So they are isolated. So a city girl may get out once a week just to get away from the kids for an hour [by coming to the group].

[Then] there are the ones that are hermits. They have no friends and no personalities. They are very isolated. They live a hermit existence. . . . [There is also] the sheltered teen group that doesn't have any information available in the schools, and their parents don't talk about it [sex and childbirth].

An additional concern for the service providers was the isolation of the teen father. "Teen fathers are more likely the ones that are looking for a place to stay . . . the ones that are homeless." Isolation, caused by a lack of transportation, rural geography, and demographics, as well as the inability to identify teen fathers, makes service delivery to this population extremely difficult. Although teen mothers are encouraged by some service providers to include their partners in doctor visits and other counseling programs, involvement by teen fathers in the present service-delivery system is minimal.

The service providers also addressed the health needs of the teen parents.

One of the obviously big concerns with teens is their nutrition during pregnancy. That is real important. A lot of them [teen mothers] come here that don't have any prenatal care, and they come at six months. An awful lot. We see a lot of teens that come in their second trimester.

In this way, service providers articulated their concern for the prenatal, nutritional, and obstetric needs of parenting teens. An additional health concern, which did not emerge in discussions with the teens, was substance abuse.

In prenatal care for moms we are seeing a lot more substance abuse from the mother in the prenatal patients, and there are some teens that fall into that category. Alcohol, cocaine—there is a lot of substance abuse. . . . It's been my experience with teens that get pregnant . . . that they usually come from alcoholic families. . . . I had one girl that I particularly remember. I think she was fourteen at the time; she couldn't live with her mom. She was living with her dad who was an alcoholic, and I couldn't get her any services from [the local mental health center] to deal with the alcohol problem—coping with it, with the father who was an alcoholic. It's real tough here. . . . We don't have an Alateen program here.

This concern about substance abuse issues leads to the additional problem of working with teen mothers under the age of fifteen. The concerns addressed in chapter 5 by the clients themselves in this regard were echoed by the service providers, who exhibited ambivalence and ambiguity when dealing with those under fifteen years old. Because youth under the age of sixteen are caught in a legal catch-22 since they are responsible for their children's health but not legally responsible for themselves, service providers often find it difficult to work with this age-group. Instead of dealing directly with the client, the service provider must work through parents, some of whom are supportive and some are not.

Well sometimes it's easier, if they live with parents or a parent who is supportive and helpful to them. . . . [I]f they are younger, they do seem to be more likely to be at home because they really can't move out until they are sixteen and it's real hard for them to do that. . . . If it is a bad family situation, [that] can present a lot of problems.

I guess I have to take a specific example of a patient that I had when I first got hired here. She was twelve going on thirteen. She just had a baby six months earlier; she's either fourteen or fifteen now. Have seen her grow up over the past three years, grow up into accepting to raise this

six-month-old child because her mother is mentally ill; and I can see the
changes in the young parents that I do see.
    I would say that emotionally, most of them are not ready for it. . . .
Their bodies . . . are not ready for the physical changes . . . they can't
accept themselves because everybody else isn't having this happen to them.
They feel, Why me? Why do I have to be different? Why is this happening
to me? I can't believe I have this stomach now and everybody is noticing
and people are talking about me.

Throughout the interview process, it was evident that the service providers had a concern for and wanted to be of assistance to
the teen parent first and, if possible, then to her family. As indicated
by the previous examples, the service providers discussed teenage
pregnancy and parenting in relationship to other issues such as alcohol and drug abuse. Noticeably absent was any discussion of teen
pregnancy as a result of incest. I did not pursue this issue either. It
wasn't until I reviewed the data at a later date that the omission
became apparent. When I reflected on this omission, the complexity of the needs of pregnant teens became obvious. The expectation
placed on service providers to meet all teenagers' needs may become
overwhelming. Adding to the complexity of the problem is the fact
that the service providers must also work within organizations and
with other organizations and agencies.

Organizational Issues

Service providers work in organizations and environments that have
bureaucratic procedures, human resource problems, political agendas, and cultural norms that affect not only the way they function
but also their self-esteem, job satisfaction, and quality of life.
    As discussed previously, the direct-service providers indicated
that the most rewarding aspect of their work was the personal satisfaction of helping a client and the most frustrating aspect of their
work was the inability to help a client. Often, organizational and
job-related difficulties contributed to this frustration. Among these
were organizational regulations (i.e., age requirements for clients,
limits on the type of service offered, and limitations on who could
be transported for services and on where and when this could take

place, heavy caseloads, and lack of resources.) When several of these factors affected the same client, the frustration increased. "We service over 200 girls part time for two days a week. . . . On one of these days they are in groups. That means that [my coworker] and I are carrying a burden of being in the office and doing the paperwork and going on home visits." With good humor, she continued, "And of course that pays so well."

It's been a rough couple of days. One thing [that makes my work difficult] is the law. They are saying at sixteen you can leave home but your parents are still financially responsible for you; we can't really do certain things for you unless we get your parents involved here. If your parents say it is O.K. and you can't live there, I guess that is the specific thing that frustrates me. I guess it would be the laws around it. . . . Part of the problem for us is the logistics here. It's how we are set up. Myself and [my coworker], you notice where we are [basement]. We have doctors one floor up, but we have doctors in the next office building over and we are constantly running. And then often what happens is when a girl [is] down there, either they get lost or they don't feel like coming all the way down. I mean it's crazy, eight months pregnant and [the girls are walking up and down steps].

Although many service providers indicated that a heavy caseload was burdensome, one governmental agency was experimenting with a reduced-load case management system. Through this program a special unit of social workers was created. These special caseworkers were recruited from volunteers within the agency who had experience with and enjoyed working with adolescent clients. These social workers had a lighter caseload than their counterparts within the same organization. This lighter caseload allowed the staff to focus their energies not only on the teen mother but also on the complete family case. In this way social workers who were not part of the special unit could get a complete family transferred to the special unit. When the teen mother was referred, the whole family case was transferred to the special unit. Through this holistic family approach, social workers believed that they had a greater depth of involvement with the teen mother and her family, which resulted in a greater impact and a greater ability to provide services. As discussed in chapter 3, this approach met with success but was on the verge of being cut because of lack of funds.

Lack of resources, which the service providers also identified as an organizational barricade to service delivery, included the lack of financial resources, which has an impact on staff hiring and salaries. They also cited lack of space for individual and group counseling, as well as office space for private phone consultations and for writing reports. This was of particular concern for outreach workers and nutrition counselors who make several phone calls. The outreach workers also cited lack of transportation and, in some cases, poor transportation arrangements in rural areas as a major deterrent to individual and group counseling as well as to recreational activities for teen mothers and their children. The organizational, financial, and legal restrictions to transporting clients proved particularly frustrating. The service providers believed that additional resources might remedy this situation.

These organizational and job-related frustrations recurred in my discussions with service providers. Despite these frustrations, the service providers generally found satisfaction in their work with teen mothers and their families.

Professional Preparation

Concern regarding professional preparation emerged indirectly from my conversations with the direct-service providers about their organizational frustrations. Within the several organizations that interacted with and referred clients to the AECYM, the service providers were from various professions. At the hospital, medically trained professionals such as doctors and nurses interacted with social workers trained in other counseling techniques. In other organizations, social workers interacted with educators, and both groups trained in profession-specific techniques and jargon such as counseling and goal setting.

Difficulties between professionals within a single organization were a significant part of the frustration felt by service providers. For example, the AECYM educators, who were generally trained to focus on the completion of specific units of study within specific periods of time, would become frustrated by their isolation from other teachers in the regular school. This posed genuine problems for the teachers, who several times made special arrangements for a student to complete her assignments only in the end to have a student drop out of school because of overwhelming social problems. These social problems were discussed with the guidance counselor, who, because of confidentiality, didn't share this information with the teacher. Over a period of weeks in the counseling office, I observed several teachers stopping in to ask the attendant aide about specific students. For example, I heard a teacher tell an attendant aide, "Here are Jane's assignments for two weeks. I prepared an assignment she can do at home instead of the one we're doing in the classroom. How's she doing?"

The attendant aide replied, "Her mom will be in this afternoon. All I know is she won't be in for two weeks."

Three days later, the teacher asked the aide, "Any news on Jane?"

"No," the attendant aide replied, "but I'm planning to stop by this afternoon."

The next day, as the teacher walked in to the office, the attendant aide told her, "I stopped by Jane's yesterday. She decided to drop out of school. She gave me these books to give you."

"What happened?"

"I'm not sure; you need to talk to one of the counselors."

Conflicts between social workers and teachers arose around situations in which a client's social or physical situation prevented her from completing her educational pursuits. As much as the teacher wanted to be supportive of the student, confidentiality prevented the social worker from discussing the case with the teacher. This proved even more frustrating for the teacher, who viewed such lack of trust as an insult to his or her profession.

Interdisciplinary tension within organizations could be addressed in the professional training programs of such service providers as nurses, social workers, teachers, and religious leaders, to mention a few. As the needs and problems of youth and their families become more complex, it is imperative that professional service providers interact with their colleagues, not only in other organizations (through a referral and a case management system) but first and foremost within their own organizations or agencies.

Interagency Cooperation

Interagency cooperation was viewed by the service providers as a significant factor in easing their job responsibilities. As indicated in an earlier discussion of the referral system, the service providers (in particular, the social workers from the various agencies) knew each other by name. They could easily call each other for an update on a client and share information between agencies because of release-of-information forms signed by the clients for just such purposes. "We work a lot with [this other agency] and they are really good about . . . sharing information . . . and getting and signing the release forms."

This rapport worked well for the social workers, who generally made referrals to other agencies. However, service providers who did not have contact with professionals outside their own agency felt isolated. This was particularly true for teachers who were working at the alternative school. The ten teachers there had limited interaction with their colleagues in the regular school on a daily basis. On the other hand, the counselors and social workers at the alternative school had regular contact with social workers and counselors in other agencies and organizations. If the teachers also experienced conflicts with, or perceived a lack of cooperation from, the counselors and social workers in their own organization, they felt even more isolated.

For service providers working with the issue of adolescent pregnancy, interagency cooperation has a dual role. It provides a referral network for client services and a support system for the service providers.

Summary

The direct-service providers are the link between the client and the service-delivery system. Their role in service delivery is critical and is influenced by several factors, including the following:

- Despite the services providers' concern and empathy for clients, pressures exerted by organizational issues, professional preparation, and interorganizational systems influence their ability to provide services to their clients.
- An organization's bureaucratic procedures, human resource

problems, political agendas, and cultural norms affect not only the way its providers function but also their self-esteem, job satisfaction, and quality of life.

- Professional preparation, training, and language create challenges in comprehensive service-delivery systems because service providers trained in various professions need to communicate with providers from other professions within their own agency or organization and from other agencies and organizations.

- Through interagency cooperation, direct-service providers have access to a referral network for clients and a support system for themselves.

Chapter Eight
The Voice of Administrators

Seventeen program administrators were interviewed. The ten females and seven males all indicated that they were surprised by the career process that had led them to their present administrative positions, although only one did not view her position as an evolutionary process within a specific professional career path. This may indicate that chance opportunities may play a more significant role in careers than careful career planning.

Fifteen of the program administrators were local people whose roots were in the community. All but one of the program administrators indicated that they were involved in community or professional activities (e.g., on the board of directors of a nonprofit agency, a member of various task forces organized around family and youth-related issues, or active in church organizations) that provided them with an opportunity to network with other agency directors, members of the community, or other professionals. All the program directors agreed that this type of networking facilitated interagency cooperation. Through these types of activities, the program directors came to know other program directors and became acquainted with the services other programs provided.

Two program administrators, however, had curtailed their outside involvement. One of these had to be extremely selective when he was asked to serve on a board of directors because, as the director of a funding agency, he could not be involved with an agency that had the potential for being funded directly or indirectly by his agency. The other program administrator had only recently been appointed to his position. The pressure of his new duties and his desire to be available to the clients in the program forced him to limit his outside involvement. In both these cases the limiting of outside, interagency activities took place after the program administrators had been in the area for a number of years and had established reputations within the community.

Although they curtailed activities that might be considered conflicts of interest, both of these administrators took on other activities, such as teaching at the local colleges, nonconflicting board appointments, and advocacy roles. In this way, all the program administrators demonstrated a community involvement that had an impact on the interagency networking within the community.

In describing a successful client intervention, the program administrators all made some statement of a long-term goal related to self-sufficiency. However, all the program administrators were aware of the difficulty in achieving and measuring such long-term goals. Instead, short, realistic goals (such as helping a client keep her doctor's appointment) were described. The major steps toward self-sufficiency were stated by one program administrator:

A teen mother that we've worked with . . . has managed to get herself situated independently in her own apartment and has established a source of income . . . and . . . she is giving some quality parenting to her child such as medical care and that bonding is happening at each stage of child development.

The program administrators saw these tasks as developmental and evolving over a long period of time, generally far beyond the duration of two- or three-year service-delivery programs. Follow-up services and programming for young parents ages eighteen to twenty-three were viewed as a next step.

Expanded programming, however, requires additional funds, and in working to establish a comprehensive service-delivery system for parenting teens, the program administrators' interests were intertwined with the funding and referral systems. The allocation of funds depended to a great extent on each program administrator's ability to manage a successful program. As the director of one funding agency remarked: "The credibility of the program administrator is important. In addition, I look for the three C's: communication, coordination, and cooperation."

It takes time for a program administrator to gain credibility, build trust, and create the networking and support system between him or her and the program administrators of other organizations, clients, and the community. This is particularly true in funding and referral systems.

The funding and referral systems were an integral part of the service-delivery system and reflected one of the primary stakes of program administration. One administrator explained:

As a funding agency our job is to help develop programs and to fill gaps in services. We are required by state law to do a needs assessment, which includes youth problem indicators such as number of pregnancies; resource indicators, that is, information on the types of services that are available and the type of clients they serve; program performance data, that is, looking at the agencies we fund to see if they are doing what they're supposed to be doing.

. . . I've been here eighteen years. . . . [W]e were funding two programs and that was it and I've seen the system grow. And it was interesting in the seventies (you know, when money was available); there was all kinds of money coming out to [be applied] for. No one wanted to work with anyone else—a place like the YMCA applied for a counselor program because the money was out there.

The eighties came on board and the money started to get less and less. We began to tell agencies, "Hey, you can't run all types of programs just because a need isn't being met. You have to concentrate on what you do best and rely on the other agencies that provide the other services to fill that gap." Since the money has dried up, it has forced the agencies to say, "Yeah, maybe you're right."

We were saying, "Hey, we're not going to fund you anymore just because you're a Y and there's a need. If we don't think you're appropriate, we're not going to fund you. . . . It makes more sense to fund an agency that is a counseling agency to provide that because, number 1, it's going to take less money to provide the same job, and the other thing that's happening is that the problems of the kids we're seeing are more severe. . . . You're not dealing with a kid who has just one or two problems; you're dealing with a kid who has a number of them: he may have a substance abuse problem and may have gotten some girl pregnant.

There's just a multiplicity of problems, and agencies are realizing they now need these other agencies.

Funding systems and referral systems were intertwined and complex. Within the referral system in this community, a delicate balance existed between the local family planning organization and a religiously affiliated charity that administered the federally funded Women, Infants, and Children (WIC) food subsidy program. The staff of the WIC program were required by law to ask every client if she needed information on family planning issues.

In tracking the source of referrals to the family planning organization, its program director stated that referrals from the WIC program were somewhat lower than expected. However, no other organization seemed concerned about the religious affiliation of the local WIC program. In fact, when program administrators were asked directly if the religious affiliation of the WIC program was a problem, they responded negatively. Most program administrators found the administration of the WIC program to be very satisfactory, given a history of mismanagement by a previous administrative organization. After all, the community almost lost the WIC program, and the religious affiliated organization stepped in and saved it.

This concern regarding referrals did not exist for the staff at the AECYM. All of the clients who were eligible for WIC services received them, as well as family planning information, which was part of the center's general counseling protocol. Therefore, as far as the clients of the AECYM were concerned, whether the WIC staff referred to the family planning clinic or not was irrelevant because the WIC received services from the center's staff. For a teen parent this questionable nonreferral would be a problem if she were not at the AECYM.

As discussed in chapter 4, the major funding agencies had created a joint funding process and a network of program administrators for funded agencies. This was helpful in comprehensive program planning for the total service-delivery system. However, if a not-for-profit agency was not funded by a major funding source, its program directors did not attend networking meetings. In the area of teenage pregnancy, this had a significant impact on the networking process.

Neither the local family planning agency nor the religiously af-filiated administrators of the WIC program attended these meet-ings. Neither program was funded by the major funding source. This lack of attendance could explain why both the directors of these organizations reported their feelings of "being on the fringe" of the networking system and their concern about a lack of contact with other program administrators.

Both these administrators were considered "new on the block." This was significant because most of the funded agency directors interviewed were long-time residents of the community and had held positions of authority for over fifteen years. When asked how an agency administrator could "break into" the funding network, the directors of the funding agencies suggested the following three crieteria: (*a*) documented need, (*b*) professionalism, and (*c*) account-ability.

In general, the program administrations had been in the com-munity for over ten years, had built up levels of trust by following through on commitments, and were known for their professional-ism. The system worked well because of this personal contact and knowledge, and this suggests that comprehensive services requires long-term support by service professionals in the community.

In summary, the program administrators contributed to the ser-vice-delivery system in the following ways:

- Networking among administrators from agencies involved in the service-delivery system was crucial to maintaining the system.
- Through their longevity as administrators within the com-munity, the program administrators had an opportunity to build credibility with their colleagues. Long-standing net-works within an agency provided a framework for interorganizational collaborative programs.
- Funding and referral systems were dependent on the pro-gram administrator's knowledge of and working relation-ships with the program administrators of the other service-delivery agencies in the area.

Chapter Nine
The Voice of Policymakers

Four local and twelve national policymakers were interviewed. I had an opportunity to attend an annual board meeting of a national organization interested in adolescent pregnancy and parenting at a national conference on adolescent pregnancy. Through my participant observer strategy, I obtained information through formal and informal interviews with the policymakers, including representatives from a government agency, and from members of a grass-roots "national network" focused on issues relating to the care and prevention of adolescent pregnancy. The interviews took place in November 1989.

For the first time in its ten-year history, the annual meeting of the national professional organization was held in Washington, D.C.[1] The individual board members were actively involved in the administration of long-standing teenage pregnancy and parenting programs, state-level administration and policymaking, or both. Some are well-known authors, consultants, and advocates whose works were well accepted by service-delivery people in the field of adolescent pregnancy; others were service-delivery professionals from around the country.

Although membership in the organization was open to the public, the membership at the time of the study had years of hands-on, practitioner-driven experience. This group, composed mostly of women, was therefore highly qualified to reflect on the state of adolescent pregnancy and parenting issues in the nation.

Based on my interviews at the national level, four areas of concern emerged: federal legislation, the developmental level of the client, the availability and use of family support structures, and the educational experiences available to parenting teens.

The policymakers reported that the implementation of the Welfare Reform Act of 1988, which required any non–high school graduate under the age of eighteen and on public assistance to attend a job-training program or enroll in a school in order to receive financial assistance, was important. The policymakers were particularly concerned with the impact this legislation had on teen parents under the age of sixteen, who have up to three years of schooling left before they complete high school.[2]

The interviewees also voiced their deep concern over the difficulties of dealing with clients who are at a developmental level where they think concretely and cannot project or realistically plan for what life will be like with a child. The lack of methods and materials available to practitioners for use with this age-group was decried. The tasks required of parenting teens under the age of fifteen was likened to the task of asking a six-month-old child to walk away from an electric socket.

The policymakers reported that the client's support system was a factor in the client's success. The interviewees stated that because of the developmental difficulties of adolescent parents under the age of fifteen, family support systems were absolutely necessary if these young parents were to complete high school. Without some type of family support, the prognosis for the teen parent was very poor.

The policymakers were concerned about the educational experiences of parenting teens. There has been a historical debate over—and therefore, fluctuating policies on—whether to mainstream parenting teens into the regular school program or to provide them with alternative, separate educational experiences that are geared toward their unique situation. Although mainstreaming parenting teens appears to address equity issues, special alternative schools address the individual needs of this group. The interviewees felt that equity did not necessarily equal appropriate services. Providing equal service to people with different needs is inequitable because one group does not have its needs met. It is important to advocate programs that meet the needs of individuals. Therefore, it is appropriate to provide an array of services and educational opportunities for young parents, so that teen mothers can choose the educational model that best meets their needs.

On the local level, the interagency cooperation exhibited in the service-delivery system was most strikingly due to the fact that the policymakers have known each other for over fifteen years. Two of the four local-level policymakers were part of the initial interagency coalition that conducted the needs assessment of the program and developed and implemented it. An advisory board member stated:

I think our organization is the pioneer. We [had] the founding role [in] having the community recognize this problem. That happened in the late sixties or early seventies. I think the stimulus at that time was the federal government: the [changes during] the sixties, the Civil Rights Act, all of those sorts of things. We had at that time what was called a county coalition. It was bringing all groups together. They were trying to bring together the government and educational institutions to face the problems. . . . So what we did through this coalition, we had a community committee and I think the original committee is the reason people say we coordinate today. . . . So what we did was we asked the school system to send representatives, public health, all of our social agencies including the Salvation Army, which was a very large representative because they were closing their Home for Unwed Mothers. Now they are opening them again in different parts of the country. I understand why that could happen. . . . So we have all these people, and we have pastors from the black churches and from the white churches—a lot of different types of people. We had some court judges, we had people from the pro-bation department . . . who were on our board of directors years ago. When I said, "Who knows about this problem and who can we get for the meeting?" everybody said, "Oh, you have to have family court and probation." But all of those people came; in fact, the family court judge who came and who is still there was a little reluctant to come to this meeting because we titled it "Services to Unmarried Mothers." . . . These people met for over a year and a half, and they consistently annexed representatives from every phase of the community and we talked about this problem. . . . [N]ot talking to the girls as you do today, the social worker who first noticed the problem brought tape recordings of what the girls said. I played those. After we had all gotten to know one an-other, after we were all comfortable with the subject, after there weren't red faces, I played those tapes at a couple of meetings. I had listened to them ahead of time. They were really revealing. Some of them were heartbreaking, and there were tears at the table. Others became angry because the girls were criticizing the departments that they were in. They were telling it, but they were telling it so from the heart that we believed them. So I think that—as often happens at these meetings most of the time—I had the head of that department, the head of probation, the family court judge (when he couldn't come, he sent his first assistant)—it's another [good] principle . . . in coordination at some level. You have the top person there because, if you don't, then it gets filtered down, things get delayed, the sensitivity, the changing of patterns never occurs. . . . Then we began to piece together what was happening to them and what they needed. I think this is another thing that kept us together—this coalition had planning people, you know, people with a real expertise for planning and public administration and all that. . . . People don't fund planners very much now.

So . . . all our information we put . . . on a circle on the board. We kept working it on the board, so this whole group together could see a picture of what we needed. It was like the whole group together said, "We need a one-site place." Because we were finding out they came from place to place, and we needed a central site. Who would give leadership to a central site? Then we really had the church battles between education. The superintendent had been a part of this. We also had the social service people, the Family and Children's organizations, the charities, people like that. I think they began to think there would be some money here someplace. We didn't yet have the money. Actually we chose the schools because of their consistent attendance at meetings and interest and because they offered to give uncharged leadership for a year till we saw how it grew and they offered us a basement home and a school that was not being used. So we chose them.

All four local policymakers articulated a belief that this personal knowledge of each other over several years prompted the trust and strong bonds that characterized this system. These policymakers headed or were indirectly connected with the organizations that provided the main services to parenting teens in the community. As with the program administrators, the local policymakers had a major stake in the funding and referral system. They also had, by virtue of the fact that their job security was dependent on reelection and re-appointment, a stake in the political system.

At least four powerful forces were at work within the political network that accompanied the service-delivery system to pregnant and parenting teens in the community: (*a*) turf issues, (*b*) the established hierarchy of local policymakers, (*c*) the lack of resources, and (*d*) the multiplicity of problems within the community.

The turf struggles stemmed from at least three boundaries: geopolitical, organizational, and job-specific.

1. *Geopolitical.* Although the AECYM was located in the city, it serviced clients from several towns located on the border between two counties. Therefore, different school districts, governing bodies, funding sources, youth programs, etc., overlapped at varying levels throughout the system. Some clients might belong to a particular school district (Board of Cooperative Educational Services) that serviced several cities in two counties. A client may attend school in one county, live in another, and go for medical treatment in both. These geographical boundaries might come into conflict within the service-delivery system.

2. *Organizational.* These were also a potential source of conflict, but the fact that very little, if any, duplication of services existed within the community minimized the effect that organizational disputes had on this system. The county was small enough that each agency was respected and recognized as the authority in its particular field.

3. *Job-related.* The importance of job-related boundaries was revealed through interviews with at least three program administrators. They discussed the personal difficulty some senior administrators had in asking for help. These three administrators felt that the senior administrators viewed asking for help or cooperating with other agencies as a personal failure, as if they had not done their job properly. If they had done the job they were hired for, they wouldn't need to ask for help. Patience, training, organizational support from superiors, pressure from peers, and constituent input were some suggestions for overcoming this barrier.

The established local hierarchy was a second powerful force within the service-delivery system. The major players in this system (that is, the project director, school district superintendent, the board president of the AECYM, and the administrators of at least two funding sources) were only some of the individuals who had been within the system for over ten years. Three of them have worked together for nearly twenty years. As mentioned in chapter 8, fifteen of the seventeen administrators interviewed had roots in the community.

The longevity that characterized this system presented local policymakers with a unique problem. The issue of "succession" created a dilemma, particularly for the program director who had been with the AECYM since it began twenty years ago. As she prepared to retire, the question of her replacement became important. Questions such as How much input should a retiree have in finding her or his replacement? Should the retiree mentor someone to take her or his place? How will the program change when the retiree leaves? How can the retiree help orchestrate these changes? and What are the political ramifications of naming a successor? would become increasingly important in the next several years, as the program administrators and local policymakers began to retire.

The opposite side of this situation was of equal concern: how were new people being brought into the established network? The interviewees were split on the question of how much, if any, effort should be made by the existing network to actively bring in new people. On the one hand, some program administrators felt that the new recruits should be responsible for initiating contact and getting to know the senior program administrators. Others felt that it was important for existing policymakers and program administrators to seek out and welcome new program administrators, and specific orientation and training were suggested for incoming service providers. This training was viewed as important because all but two of the program administrators and local policymakers "came up through the ranks" within the area and their present organization.

The third and fourth forces within the political network, the lack of resources, and the multiplicity of problems within the community, were actually seen by the program administrators as powerful tools in encouraging interagency cooperation among vying political forces. One policymaker went into great detail on how the local constituency brought pressure to bear on a local politician to become part of the joint process to secure additional funding for the community to help deal with the problems faced by local youth.

In the complexity of this service-delivery system, the policymakers carried a responsibility for establishing policies on both the national and local levels. They created an atmosphere conducive to interagency cooperation, which leads to comprehensive services for pregnant and parenting teens.

Notes

1. The purpose of my national-level research was to determine the major concerns regarding the service-delivery system to parenting teens and to guide the local research. The focus of this research was to determine how services were delivered to adolescent parents; it was not intended to be a complete analysis of the national policy toward adolescent pregnancy. Several authors, including Vinovskis (1988) and Hayes (1987), discuss the history of the political development of governmental agencies focusing on adolescent pregnancy issues, and therefore, they will not be discussed here.

2. The policymakers stated that it would be difficult for a teen mother to complete her education or work given the lack of day care and transportation and the other barriers faced by teen mothers. The information presented here reflects the state of the national welfare debate in 1989–90. See chapter 15 for an update.

Chapter Ten
Summary and Recommendations

As I reviewed the data, my motto emerged: Adolescent parenting is not a problem to be solved but a reality to be lived. Providers and policies that enhance the teen parents' ability to live their lives in a caring environment are the appropriate models for service delivery.[1] This is not to say that problem solving is not an important aspect of service delivery. However, problem solving is only a subset of life. Every service-delivery system needs to treat the parenting teen as a worthwhile human being and not as a statistical problem. From this holistic orientation, dynamic answers are provided for the following questions: Do gaps in service exist? What models of service delivery lessen these gaps? How do individuals within the system cope with changing policies? What linkages between individuals and organizations create a comprehensive service-delivery system? Each question is explored in this chapter.

The Whole Picture

In answer to the question Do gaps in service exist? the descriptions provided in chapters 3 to 9 demonstrate the importance of viewing the service-delivery system as a total system, incorporating the whole picture. My study is a departure from most other studies on the issues of service delivery to parenting teens, which have generally focused on the individual components and stakeholders of the service-delivery system. In my attempt to focus on the entire system from the viewpoint of each of the various stakeholders (especially the teen parent), it has become evident that the phrase "gaps in service" has different meanings depending upon what kind of and how much service the stakeholders (including clients) believe clients should receive.

If a person believes that the basic needs such as food, clothing, and shelter are to be provided, then the service-delivery system was very adequate at the Alternative Education Center for Young Mothers (AECYM), since the clients I interviewed stated that all of these needs were being adequately met with the exception of difficulties in receiving utility service and during transitional living arrangements. Without these basic services, some clients and their children could have been added to the ranks of the homeless.

If, however, a person believes that in addition to the basic needs, health needs should also be met, then a gap in services did exist. The clients indicated that they had very adequate care while pregnant but that once their child was born, they did not have a doctor for their own needs. Pediatricians were available for their children, but difficulties arose when the teen mother needed care for herself that was not related to pregnancy. However, the clients also indicated that either their mental health needs were either adequately being met or they knew where to secure these services if they were needed.

If a person believes that in addition to such basic needs as food, clothes, and shelter, health needs, education, and life skills (including day care and transportation) are part of the service-delivery system, the gap in service widens. The clients indicated that a complex pattern of transportation, day care, and job training or employment challenges existed. Without all these pieces working together, any one was difficult to arrange. The system worked well for those parenting teens enrolled in the AECYM. It worked less well for (a) those in outreach areas where problems of transportation were a particular concern, (b) clients who had dropped out of school, or (c) clients who had graduated. In other words, the farther away a client was from the central hub of the services, the more difficult it was for her to receive services.

If one believes that the service-delivery system should also encompass what the director referred to as "soft skills," the gap in service widens even further. Soft skills refer to issues of quality of life and can be characterized by a single word: relationship. Clients, service providers, program administrators, and policymakers were all concerned with this issue. Ellen was concerned with an interior relationship with a "higher power" in her life. The husband of a teen mother was concerned with receiving counseling "to get some idea of what she was going through" and to understand their relationship.

The teen mothers indicated that their relationship with their child was their greatest joy. The service providers stated that their relationship with their clients was the most rewarding aspect of their work, and they were also concerned about their relationship with other service providers. The program administrators discussed the importance of knowing the other program administrators, of having a personal relationship with them based on trust and built on years of accountable interaction.

Although every stakeholder group discussed the importance of relationships, this issue is far from having been addressed adequately. The first question to be considered is whether the discussion and inclusion of program components dealing with relationships are appropriate for organized service delivery. The answer is that establishing and maintaining "soft skills" is indeed a legitimate priority based on Weatherly, Levine, Perlman, and Kleiman's (1986) conclusion that the caring professional is the key component to a successful service-delivery system.

Mayeroff (1971) defines *caring* as follows:

[H]elping another grow and actualize himself is a process, a way of relating to someone that involves development, in the same way that friendship can only emerge in time through mutual trust and a deepening and qualitative transformation of the relationship.

Given this definition of caring, the question becomes, How can such relationships be developed? In the service-delivery system studied, some of these relational needs had already been addressed in a formal way. For example, the client's relationship with her child was directly addressed through the day care center.

Counselors and clients discussed the client's relationship with the baby's father. In the senior civics class the students participated in activities that focused on their participation in society. Service providers discussed their relationships with the clients in staff meetings. Despite these efforts, however, gaps in service existed once again for those clients farthest removed from the center of the service-delivery system. For example, clients who were part of the outreach program did not have extensive services that helped them relate to their children, clients who had graduated from high school and who were no longer attending the AECYM no longer received counseling, and teen fathers and the parents of teen parents received little or no support through the existing service-delivery system in understanding their relationships with the teen mother and her child.

If services are viewed as a hierarchy, then clients who were enrolled in the AECYM were receiving the full spectrum of services available; those in the outreach program had fewer opportunities for these services; those who had graduated had even less. The largest gap in services existed for those who had dropped out of school.

Another gap in services was that neither the AECYM nor the Department of Social Services Case Management (DSSCMS), part of the AECYM referral system, provided consistent ongoing services for clients in their late teens and early twenties, when teen mothers often have second and third children. The DSSCMS was beginning to address this problem with a program for young mothers above high school age.

I do not mean to imply that because gaps in service exist, something is wrong with the system. The opposite is true. Something is very right with the system for those who participate in it. The system needs to reach out even farther than it does at present, to include additional clients and additional services. To cut any aspect of the existing program would only widen the gap. It has taken this service-delivery system twenty years to build up its program to the present level.[2]

Caring in the Delivery of Services

In answer to the question What models of service delivery lessen gaps in services? it became evident through this fieldwork that a model that allows the provider to establish a caring relationship with the client is the most effective. This model can vary in structure as long as it allows the provider who works directly with the client sufficient discretion to develop an ongoing and supportive rapport.

Mayeroff's (1971) discussion of seven characteristics of caring (knowledge, patience, honesty, trust, humility, hope, and courage) serves to organize this analysis of caring. The local service delivery systems studied, particularly the DSSCMS and the AECYM, demonstrated these characteristics.

Knowledge

Mayeroff emphasizes a knowledge of client needs: "In order to care I must understand the other's needs and I must be able to respond properly to them" (Mayeroff 1971, 9). When a client was enrolled in the AECYM and the DSSCMS, a needs assessment was conducted. In the DSSCMS, the needs assessment was even broader because it incorporated the teen parent's family as a single unit. The clients interviewed mentioned both the DSSCMS and the AECYM as supportive organizations that met their needs and in which they found caring service providers.

Patience

Patience is an important ingredient in caring: "I enable the other to grow in its own time and in its own way. . . . Patience includes tolerance of a certain amount of confusion and floundering. . . . Tolerance expresses my respect for the growth of the other and my appreciation of the 'wastefulness' and free play that characterize growth" (Mayeroff 1971, 12–13).

Many service-delivery systems have rules and regulations that mitigate against patience with clients. This was not the case at the AECYM or the DSSCMS. At the AECYM clients had ongoing access to counselors, teachers, and the program director. Teachers would prepare assignments materials for absent students, even when the students had been absent several times or dropped out of school; outreach workers would transport clients to and from group meetings; the program director would "waste" time conversing with clients and developing a rapport with them. In the DSSCMS, the caseloads of the service providers were lower than those of general departmental caseworkers specifically to allow case managers the opportunity to spend more time with each client.

Honesty

"In caring I am honest in trying to see truly. To care for the other I must see the other as it is and not as I would like it to be. . . . I must be genuine in caring for the other. I must 'ring true'" (Mayeroff

1971, 13–14). The AECYM was particularly designed to see parenting teens simply as adolescent mothers, that is, as junior and senior high school students who had the added responsibility of motherhood. Therefore, their particular needs (such as child care and transportation) were addressed. Furthermore, the staff at the AECYM was trained in adolescent issues normally found in regular high school settings. The reading level of the materials used in child care classes was geared for the adolescent reader as opposed to the adult mother. It was this very characteristic (that is, seeing the client as having needs specific to teen parenthood) that prompted local policymakers to create the AECYM twenty years ago.

Trust

"Caring involves trusting the other to grow in its own time and in its own way. . . . I trust him to make mistakes and to learn from them" (Mayeroff 1971, 14–15). The clients viewed the teachers as very caring because they took the time to explain the lessons; they did not just pass students or gloss over the fact that a student didn't know an assignment. The development of trust takes time; service-delivery systems that are plagued by rapid turnover in staff have difficulty establishing client rapport. This was not the case at the AECYM or the DSSCMS. In the AECYM, the director had made a conscious effort to gradually upgrade counselor salaries in order to maintain qualified staff. The staff had remained relatively stable over the last few years. In the DSSCMS, the staff was selected from volunteers who had previous experience with adolescents.

Mayeroff mentions another aspect of trust that has an impact on service delivery: "Besides trusting the other, I must also trust my own capacity to care. . . . Continuing preoccupation with whether my actions are correct indicates lack of trust in myself and in focusing attention on myself, makes for further indifference to the needs of the others" (Mayeroff 1971, 16). This preoccupation with self was not evident in any of the programs I visited. Although problems or treatment decisions were discussed at weekly staff meetings, I saw no evidence of any fear on the part of the staff members that they were not trusted by the program administrators.[3] In other words, the trust the service providers had in the clients was echoed by the trust the program administrators had in the service providers. Therefore, the service providers were not burdened with the pressure to perform perfectly in order to maintain their positions. This was particularly true at the DSSCMS, where policies and procedures were developed by the entire staff.

Humility

"Caring involves continuous learning about the other; there is always something more to learn. The man who cares is genuinely humble in being ready and willing to learn more about the other and himself, and what caring involves. . . . No source is felt to be beneath me in principle: I am not humiliated to learn from any source, including my own mistakes" (Mayeroff 1971, 16–17). This characteristic of caring was exhibited through the referral system. Staff members from various organizations referred clients to other programs. Although there was some tension between the professions in the AECYM, there was a willingness on the part of the program administrator to deal with problems through staff meetings and the creation of an attendance officer's position to bridge the gap. In other words, there was a willingness to develop workable solutions.

Hope

"Hope, as an expression of a present alive with possibilities, rallies energies and activates our powers . . . for hope implies that there is or could be something worthy of commitment" (Mayeroff 1971, 19). It was the development of this sense of worth through an inner personal experience that prompted Ellen, a former teen parent, to pursue an active life of community involvement and civic responsibility as an AECYM board member and finance professional. Ellen also attributed this sense of worth to the caring attitude of the service providers at the AECYM, who supported her in her life circumstance and did not view her as a problem. This attitude of viewing clients as worthwhile and as having many possibilities before them was evident in the counseling office—where information regarding universities, colleges, and two-year community colleges was made available to the students—and in the main office, where students worked as interns. The attitude that clients were resourceful, worthwhile individuals with viable, worthwhile futures and temporarily in need of extra support provided the clients with the last characteristic, courage.

Courage

"Trust in the other to grow and in my own ability to care gives me courage to go into the unknown" (Mayeroff 1971, 20). Such courage was demonstrated twenty years ago when the AECYM was first created. For the sake of the clients, the initial group of supporters were willing to face the risks involved with starting a new program. It continues to be demonstrated by the clients in the service-delivery system as they come daily to school carrying their books, babies, bottles, and child care paraphernalia, hoping to complete high school and to go on to college or to become gainfully employed.

The AECYM: A Caring Service-Delivery System

The seven characteristics of caring point to a service-delivery model that

- Is focused on the process of personal growth and development.
- Trusts decisions to be made at the client service provider level, where the individuals within the system are trusted to utilize funds and resources appropriately.
- Tolerates mistakes as part of the growing process and is not punitive.
- Provides a continuum of service that is based on the needs of the client for as long as she needs the service, while it assists her in gaining self-sufficiency.

The AECYM was an example of a caring service-delivery system and can serve as a general model of comparison by which other communities can begin to improve their current programs or start new ones.

Networking and Interdisciplinary Cooperation

How do individuals within the service-delivery system cope with changing policies? Through my interviews, my observations of the participants, and my surveys, it became evident that one way individuals coped with change was through support networks. Tensions arose over interdisciplinary boundaries rather than organizational boundaries.

Support networks were used to varying degrees at all levels of service delivery except among the family support members (the husbands or parents of the teen parent). Clients used support networks for gathering information when their life situation changed as a result of their pregnancy. The clients also indicated that familial support was one of the key factors in sustaining them throughout their pregnancy and as young parents. Particularly for the very youngest parents, those under the age of fifteen, consistent, ongoing support was crucial.

The support was practically nonexistent for the familial support people themselves. The parents of teen parents, as well as teen fathers and other individuals who provided support for clients, needed support. Further research into the development, implementation, and evaluation of support networks for the individuals who provide support to parenting teens needs to be conducted.

At the opposite end of the service-delivery spectrum, policymakers used a national organization on adolescent pregnancy and parenting as a means of coping with the changing federal legislation regarding welfare reform and to discuss changes in the field of adolescent pregnancy and parenting. Program administrators used the established funding network to explore changing funding policies and to discover emerging community needs. If program administrators were not part of any existing funding network, they developed their own.

A support system was most crucial at the service provider's level. Service providers were the link between the client and the system. Because of this key position, their coping strategies were important to the total functioning of the service-delivery system.

In the delivery system studied, providers coped with the daily flux and change of clients, new regulations, and other circumstances by using the referral system and professional networking. The counselors at AECYM used the referral network not only to assist clients in acquiring necessary services but also as a way of securing information regarding changes at other agencies. Because counselors from the AECYM could readily call upon counselors who worked with the same clients at other agencies (e.g., WIC, DSSCMS, Catholic Charities), a network of support existed between these individuals that was not available to the teachers at the AECYM.

The teachers at the AECYM were isolated because they were the only educators who worked directly with parenting teens in the community. Although they might interact with the regular teachers on some subject matter, or with grade-level teachers at other schools, the unique experience of working with the parenting teen could not be shared with other educators. The only outlet for the teachers to other individuals who worked with parenting teens in other organizations and agencies was the counselors. The counselors had a handle on the life situation of the client both through direct contact and through the referral network. Because of the issues of confidentiality and training, the teachers at the AECYM sometimes experienced a sense not only of isolation but also of hopelessness and frustration because of this lack of interaction.

The tension between teachers and social workers stemmed not only from the interdisciplinary training difference but also from the lack of a support network for the teachers. In the service-delivery system studied, teachers were the only group of direct-service providers who did not have a support network. Except for the teachers and familial support individuals, support networks were evident at all levels of the service-delivery system and were essential to the successful functioning of the system.

Communication

What linkages between individuals and organizations create a comprehensive service-delivery system? My field research revealed a comprehensive system fostered by free and uncoerced communication among the organizations and individuals involved in the system. After a brief review of the characteristics of a comprehensive service-delivery system, Forrester's (1983) four criteria for communication (comprehension, trust, consent, and knowledge) will be used to discuss the importance of communication in the system.

Based on the Adolescent Health Services and Pregnancy Prevention Act (PL 95-626, Health Services and Centers Amendments of 1978), Weatherly, Levine, Perlman, and Kleiman (1987) defined a comprehensive service-delivery system as one that provides the following core services either in a single setting or by means of a linked referral network:

1. Pregnancy testing, maternity counseling, and referral
2. Family planning
3. Primary and preventive health services including prenatal and postnatal care
4. Nutrition information and counseling
5. Adoption counseling and referral services
6. Educational services in sexuality and family life
7. Screening and treatment for venereal disease
8. Pediatric care
9. Educational and vocational services
10. Other health services

The local service-delivery system, with the AECYM as its hub, provided all these services either at the local site or through a referral network. This system was viewed by both present and former clients as adequate, and therefore, the information on how these components were linked is useful for developing other programs.

Individual and organizational patterns of communication seemed to be the critical link for the success of this system. Forrester's conditions for "free and un-coerced communication"—comprehension, trust, consent, and truth—can be incorporated into this discussion.

Comprehension

Comprehension is defined by clear presentation, clear attribution of responsibility, and attention to significant issues. In the delivery system studied, a clear definition of roles and responsibilities existed both at the individual and organizational levels. Through the referral system, not only did the direct providers know each other, but they also knew the services that different organizations could provide for their clients. New providers were trained in the referral system through orientation meetings and site visits.

Clients indicated that they knew where to get the services they needed. Family support members were also aware of the services that were available and felt comfortable in assisting the teen parents in securing those services. Program administrators indicated that in general they knew the joint funding process used in the community and which organizations provided particular services.

It is evident, therefore, that a high level of comprehension existed throughout the service-delivery system. Information was clearly presented to and freely shared by clients, their support members, service providers, program administrators, and policymakers. This clear information sharing and understanding were essential to the successful functioning of the referral system and the ability of clients to receive necessary services.

Trust

Forrester links trust to the ability of participants within a community to listen to one another and to develop confidence in the assurances given by a particular individual or organization. Trust among the individuals in the service-delivery system has already been discussed in the section of this chapter titled "Caring in the Delivery of Services."

It is important, however, to point out the organizational assurances on which this delivery system depends. One of the funding administrators discussed the importance of accountability and professionalism based on documented need. These characteristics, as well as the fact that the program administrators and policymakers had known each other for a number of years, enabled trust to develop within this system.

Consent

Forrester describes consent as stemming from a legitimacy established by operating through procedures that are understood by and available to all the constituencies within a community. Two examples of this type of consent can be observed in the service-delivery system studied. In the referral system and the funding system, participants consented to the system by choosing to work within it. In terms of referrals, providers not only knew the services and the contact person for each service, but they also introduced new providers to the referral system through orientation sessions.

The continued use of a joint funding process for the regional and local United Ways and Youth Bureaus was possible because of the willingness of the program administrators. All the program administrators interviewed knew and were very satisfied with the funding procedures. Communication within the system therefore operated with the consent of these participants.

Truth

Forrester states that truth depends on the accurate presentation of the facts and on the participants' belief that the facts are true. The behavior of the participants at all levels of the service-delivery system depended on their belief that the information they received within the system was accurate. For example, clients generally followed up on the referral information they were given by the service providers, while program administrators relied on the day care providers' information on the availability of bed space.

Lack of Information

Lack of information, as opposed to misinformation, was viewed by the service providers as a barrier to communication. The issue of confidentiality presented a problem for teachers and was the source of tension between teachers and social workers. The teachers believed that they were not always given complete information concerning the client and that, therefore, vital information was missing. This lack of information was not perceived as a lie but as a deliberate evasion on the part of the counselors.

The tensions that arose between teachers and social workers was an example of how poor communication can make service delivery difficult, but this was but one example of poor communication in an otherwise sophisticated system of service delivery that, as a whole, operated within the four criteria mentioned by Forrester for successful communication in community planning.

Caring and Communication in the Service-Delivery System

We have to pay the closest attention to what we say. What patients say tells us what to think about what hurts them; and what we say tells us what is happening to us—what we are thinking and what may be wrong with us. Their story, yours, mine—it's what we all carry with us on this trip we take, and we owe it to each other to respect our stories and learn from them. (Coles 1989, 30)

This quote describes the attitude of listening necessary for physicians to help their patients and themselves grow and develop. It also describes the type of listening needed for developing the caring attitude discussed by Mayeroff (1971) and Kelsey (1981).

The service-delivery system studied demonstrated the characteristics of caring identified by Mayeroff and the communication techniques described by Forrester. Through this attitude of caring communication, the service providers, program administrators, and policymakers had created an environment in which service delivery to pregnant and parenting teens was viewed as supportive but in need of expansion. Through this service-delivery system, parenting teens were learning to become responsible parents who cared for themselves and their children. In this way, the service-delivery system that operated out of the AECYM fulfilled the following mandate by Mayeroff:

To help another person grow is at least to help him to care for something or someone apart from himself and it involves encouraging and assisting him to find and create areas of his own in which he is able to care. Also it is to help that other person to come to care for himself, and by becoming responsive to this own need to care to become responsible for his own life. (Mayeroff 1971, 7)

Correlates of Effectiveness

In the process of examining in depth the nuances and complexities involved in a single system, three characteristics of an effective service-delivery model became especially evident: strong leadership, interagency cooperation, and support for caring professionals.

Strong Leadership

Strong leadership based on accountability and professionalism was a key component of the service-delivery system studied. From the initial stages of development, strong individual leadership was evident despite the fact that a shift in organizational leadership occurred: A community agency task force was responsible for the initial planning of the program, but the responsibility for its implementation shifted to the school district. Those individuals involved in program development were interested in creating the best environment in which clients could receive services. The task force leaders were supported by their members because of their dedication and commitment to parenting teens. The trust developed between individuals in the initial task force helped greatly when the leadership shifted to the school. The issue concerning all was not which organization initiated the program but rather which organization was best suited to implement its goals. Some of the task force members were also involved in the school. There were personal links, and the task force easily shifted responsibility to people who had demonstrated their ability to act responsibly and professionally.

This trust and mutual respect had continued over a twenty-year period and was enhanced perhaps by the continuous service of the director, who had been present during the formative stages of the program. This leadership based on trust appeared to be critical to the program's ongoing success. The fact that the program director could bridge organizational and disciplinary boundaries through personal contacts and professional expertise was, in the view of many respondents, a key factor in the effective delivery of services to parenting teens. Questions about leadership and the antecedents of strong leadership should be examined in planning and implementing any human service program.

Interagency Cooperation

Interagency cooperation based on free and uncoerced communication and demonstrated through information sharing, referral, and support networks at various levels of interorganizational collaboration was a second prominent characteristic of this system. As noted earlier, this interagency cooperation was based on the fact that most of the direct-service providers in this system knew each other by name and generally shared program information and made client referrals across organizational lines. The ease with which information was shared on the service provider level was also evident at the program administration level, where most administrators met at least monthly in meetings conducted by the funding agencies. In addition, regular contact between people in the central service-delivery hub, as well as the ability of the direct-service providers to place a face with a name, was a key factor in the effective operation of the referral system.

Support for Caring Professionals

Support for caring professionals was manifested in a variety of ways. At this school the availability of resources (salary increases, low caseloads, and the development of organizational norms that allowed the service providers to utilize their professional expertise and discretion in job performance) was especially important. Since the caring attitude exhibited by the direct-service providers was seen by the parenting teens as essential to their success, it is logical to assume that programs that support their professionals will be more likely to retain personnel who can support clients. The local program described in this research made resources available to the service providers in numerous ways, including the allocation of appropriate space, an understanding of the time constraints in outreach and home visit travel, the provision of equipment and office supplies, and clerical support.

The program administrators were cognizant of salary issues and made efforts to raise salaries to competitive levels whenever possible to eliminate rapid turnover, while they simultaneously tried to lower caseloads so that service providers could focus in depth on individual cases over longer periods of time. Organizational norms were devised to encourage referral networking and casework meetings and to minimize paperwork. These concrete strategies proved effective in helping service providers to complete their responsibilities and in creating an atmosphere conducive to caring relationships with clients.

Recommendations

These correlates of an effective service-delivery system can be used as a guideline for other service systems. However, each service-delivery system does exist around a particular issue and around clients with specific needs. The following recommendations represent an effort to apply the general principles discussed to the specific issues that affect parenting teenagers and their families:

- *A single caseworker should remain with a young teen parent for a period of years.* Every effort should be made to provide the youngest teen parents (under the age of fifteen) with a strong and consistent support system. This recommendation is based on the fact that although the types of services required by young parenting teens are similar to those required by older teens, young teens require them for a longer period of time and in greater depth.

- *Funding for existing programs needs to be maintained.* The system studied provided adequate care for the basic needs of most clients. However, that does not mean that the service providers have succeeded in a way that renders the programs unnecessary. This research cannot stress enough the belief of the clients interviewed that without the present services and direct service providers' insights and supports, they would be unable to cope and would be overwhelmed by their situation as teen parents.

- *The basic services available to young parents of high school age need to be extended to transitional young parents eighteen to twenty-three years of age.* These clients are low-income couples or single parents who have graduated from high school and are no longer eligible for dropout or training programs. Without support, this group of parents could slide into poverty at precisely the point at which they should be able to emerge from it.

- *An effort should be made to support the living arrangements each client chooses as most conducive to raising her family.* A client who wishes to remain part of an extended family (living in her parental home or with her husband) should be allowed to do so without being penalized financially. In turn, the support for a client who wishes to be the head of a single-parent home should be sufficient for her to maintain her household.

- *Creative ways for supporting the "significant others" in the teen parents' lives need to be encouraged.* Self-help groups for the parents of teen parents, counseling for support people, and parenting classes for males were among the suggestions proposed by the family support members interviewed.

- *Recreational and leisure activities sponsored by the local ser-vice-delivery agency alone or in conjunction with other com-munity agencies should be expanded.* Creative ways of pro-viding day care and baby-sitting for these activities is central to their success.
- *Programs to encourage the development of soft skills need to be developed and implemented.* The introduction of an art thera-pist to counseling programs, field trips, involvement with fine arts programs in the community, and a renewed em-phasis on how teen parents can be of service to others in the community through volunteerism and civic awareness were some of the programs mentioned by the interviewees.

Notes

1.   The focus of this study has been on the service-delivery system to parenting teens. This is not a study of prevention services.
2.   This criticism of gaps in service should not be used to dismantle or lessen exist-ing levels of service in any way. Changes in the service-delivery system should only be added to *enhance* existing services, so that the whole picture of service delivery can be available to all clients and their families.
3.   Behaviors such as (a) differences between statements made by service provid-ers during private interviews and those made in the presence of the administra-tor, (b) requests for secrecy, and (c) abrupt behavioral changes brought on by the presence of a program administrator are some of the indicators of fear or lack of trust.

Part III

Models of Alternative Education Programs for Pregnant and Parenting Teens

Chapter Eleven
Alternative Education

A basic assumption throughout this book has been that completion of high school is an important goal for pregnant and parenting teens and that as a society we need to encourage pregnant and parenting teens to complete their education. Let's look at this assumption and ask, Why do we want pregnant and parenting teens to complete their education? How we answer this question in large part depends on how we view the purpose of education.

If education is viewed as preparation for the work force, then encouraging pregnant and parenting teens to complete their education means that we would like them to secure jobs upon graduation and, to extend this goal further, we would like to see them being financially self-sufficient. If education is viewed as general preparation for engagement in the life process, we would expect that after graduation teen parents would have the skills to solve everyday problems in their personal relationships, societal obligations, financial deals, and other aspects of everyday life. If education is viewed as the general pursuit of knowledge, then upon graduation pregnant and parenting teens should be equipped with the tools for lifelong earning.

These are only a few ways that one may look at the purpose of education. There are many more. Answers to these questions determine program development and the implementation and evaluation of schools, including alternative schools.

However, another question arises: Is there a special reason for pregnant and parenting teens to complete their education that is somehow connected with their status as parents? Does the fact that they are parents or parents-to-be somehow make it more important or somehow more necessary for them, as compared to the average student, to receive an education? If so, why?

The answers to these questions help to determine, among other things, (*a*) whether a community establishes an alternative education program for pregnant and parenting teens within their school system, (*b*) the focus of the program, (*c*) attendance and implementation guidelines, and (*d*) the program's components and requirements. These are not idle questions, nor are the answers unimportant. Throughout the history of education, communities have grappled with the purposes of education, the right of a child to an education, and the obligations of a community to educate its citizenry.

Alternative education has had a long history in this country. From part-time schools for working youth to alternative schools for dropout prevention, alternative schools have been part of our educational framework since the early 1900s (Kelly 1993). Alternative schools have been known by a variety of names, such as continuation schools, learning centers, schools within schools, open schools, magnet schools, charter schools, and multicultural schools (Young 1990). The continuation school has had a long history of serving youth who do not fit into the conventional school of the time. Continuation schools have provided youths with an opportunity to continue their education in special programs despite limitations defined by various criteria (employment, pregnancy, and juvenile delinquency), which change over time. Despite the varying criteria used to separate students into such schools, one aspect of continuation and alternative schools has remained constant. Students in the alternative schools have been defined as "misfits within the conventional schooling system [who] had either dropped out or been pushed out" (Kelly 1993, 53).

Alternative schools are often distinguished from their conventional counterparts by—

- A greater responsiveness to perceived educational needs within the community.
- A more focused instructional program, usually featuring a particular curriculum emphasizing instructional method or school climate.
- A more student-centered philosophy. Emphasis is on the whole student. Affective as well as cognitive needs are met.

- A greater autonomy. Principals, teachers, and students have greater freedom from the central administration than their counterparts.
- A smaller school and a more personalized relationship between student and staff. (Young 1990, 2–3)

Alternative schools are characterized by an emphasis on individual learning styles, flexible scheduling, team teaching, cooperative and community-based learning, individualized instruction, mentoring, and behavioral modification. In addition, effective public alternative schools have, according to Young (1990), the following characteristics:

- *Positive student-teacher relationships.* Students can talk about nonacademic as well as academic subject matter with teachers.
- *Student-centered curriculum.* Instruction is related to the student's personal experiences.
- *Varied roles for teachers.* Teachers serve as advisors, attendance officers, and guidance counselors, to meet a variety of student needs.
- *Noncompetitive classrooms.* Peer cooperation and sharing are emphasized. Positive relationships among students are encouraged.
- *Clear mission.* Schools target their students and tailor programs to fit students' needs.
- *School size.* Schools are small enough to allow students to feel part of a group, and yet they are large enough to provide necessary resources.

Despite the various efforts made by teachers and administrators in alternative education to help support youth and their families by providing programs for youth disenfranchised by the traditional school system,

Public alternative education is not El Dorado. More choice and a variety of better schools will not eliminate poverty, illiteracy, teenage drug abuse or crime. The causes of these problems involve long-standing and

complex political, social, and economic factors. Solutions to these problems must be found outside public education in the political and economic institutions of our society. (Young 1990, 126)

Teenage Pregnancy and Alternative Education

In the 1960s pregnant and parenting teenagers began to be viewed as a special population who required alternative schooling. Up until this time pregnant and parenting teenage girls were found in general alternative school settings that accepted both males and females who were viewed as unable or unwilling to function in a normal school setting. As the alternative education programs for pregnant and parenting teens emerged, several different ways of providing services for this population were tried; some continue today with new variations. Alternative schools in general—and those designed for pregnant and parenting teens, in particular—were created to serve youth with specific needs; in part, they became social agencies to compensate for disadvantages these youth may have brought with them to school (Young 1990, 28). For pregnant and parenting teens this meant, among other things, special counseling services, child care, medical care, or a combination of the three.

Alternative education programs for pregnant and parenting teens have the same characteristics as other alternative schools, and they are plagued by some of the same policy trade-offs.

The AECYM as an Alternative School

At the AECYM, the characteristics identified by Wehlage (1983) existed, as the following demonstrates:

- *Positive student-teacher relations.* The students in the alternative school described their relationships (discussed in chapter 10) as caring and supportive.
- *Student-centered curriculum.* The teachers in the program were required to teach the curriculum supplied by the state and the school district, but their teaching techniques and procedures were flexible. The focus on traditional course work met the needs of pregnant and parenting teens who wanted to finish high school and receive the necessary Carnegie units for admission to college. In addition, course

work meeting the special needs of the pregnant and parenting teens was designed. For example, child care courses were included in the curriculum.

- *Varied roles for teachers.* Teachers in the alternative school took on additional roles, for example, taking students on field trips.

- *Noncompetitive classrooms.* One of the attractive features of the alternative school, according to the students who were interviewed in the study, was the lack of competitiveness, which was due in particular to the single-gender nature of the school. The young women cited the lack of competitiveness with their male counterparts as a positive benefit.

- *Clear mission.* The mission of the alternative school was clear: Participants were expected to complete their high school education, and the necessary services (such as transportation and child care) were provided to assist students in attaining this goal.

- *School size.* The alternative school had only sixty students enrolled in the in-school portion of the program.

Trade-offs in Alternative Schools
Coed vs. Single-Sex Schools

Alternative schools for pregnant and parenting teens generally focus on the teen mother and her child. This single-sex schooling arrangement has certain benefits. The pregnant and parenting teens interviewed during the study indicated that in some ways they enjoyed being in a school without males. They did not have to worry about male-female relationships during the school day and could focus on their schoolwork. They also enjoyed interacting with other teen mothers, discussing problems, making arrangements for sharing baby-sitting, etc. What they missed were some school functions and their friends from their regular school.

Stigmatization vs. Specialization

Does attendance at an alternative school heighten one's stigmatization as a teen parent and emphasize parenthood too much as the defining characteristic of a student's life? Or does attendance at a specialized school enhance a student's sense of specialness because a school is designed to meet the particular needs of students who are parents? Some students interviewed in this study indicated that they felt stigmatized in their regular school, where they stood out as being different, and were more comfortable in a school with other teen parents. Most enjoyed the special attention of teachers that resulted from attendance at the alternative school. For a few, it was the first time they had talked with a teacher.

Academic Excellence

This is perhaps one of the most significant areas in which some alternative schools for pregnant and parenting teens fall short. Although the quality of teaching, small class size, and individual instruction enhance the learning process and help the student finish high school, the class offerings often fall short of what is available at the regular school. This lack of course offerings may be a limiting factor for young teen mothers interested in pursuing college careers. As more and more colleges begin to provide day care and other services for parents attending college, the opportunities for teen mothers to gain a college education are increasing. However, if teen mothers are forced to attend alternative schools where course offerings are limited, they will have more difficulty in gaining entrance to college. In the past, when college was more unattainable for young parents, the argument could have been made that completion of high school was more important than preparation for college. Given the increasing number of older students who have children and are returning to college, the teen parent may find college to be a possibility. Teen parenting may no longer be the educational dead end it once was thought to be if parenting teens have access to college preparatory classes. This may be a flight of fancy on my part, but during my interviews with teen parents, several indicated a desire to attend college and bemoaned the fact that some science courses were not available to them.

Re-entry into the Regular School vs. Continued Enrollment in an Alternative School

Once a student is enrolled in an alternative school, her re-entry into the regular classroom may prove problematic or at least disruptive. Recent research (Bogenschneider, Small, Riley n.d.) indicates that young people are more prone to risk-taking behavior during school transitions. Switching schools is a transition that may cause stress and feelings of ambivalence, awkwardness, and disassociation, all of which may create challenges for the student. Add to this the stress of finding out that one was pregnant, dealing with the decisions associated with early pregnancy and the physical aspects of the pregnancy itself, and the relational issues associated with the onset of parenthood, and it becomes clear that moving a student to unfamiliar surroundings may be unbearable for her.

If a young person chooses to attend an alternative school designed to meet her particular pregnancy and early parenting needs, the choice to be in a specific environment may help to alleviate some of that stress. If, on the other hand, a student is required to attend an alternative program, the mandatory nature of attendance may add to the already stressful event of pregnancy, even if the program is designed to meet the physical needs created by the pregnancy.

Another factor to consider is the length of stay in an alternative school. Sometimes a school district may require a pregnant student to attend an alternative school as soon as a pregnancy is revealed to the school personnel; other districts require attendance only from the third trimester. Some districts require re-entry into the regular school two weeks after the birth of the child, and other districts allow students to remain in an alternative setting for several years until their graduation.

Given that transitions between school settings can cause stress for young mothers, the trade-off of creating additional stress as a result of re-entry into the regular class must be balanced against the benefits of attendance in the regular classroom. What can the young mother gain by being back in the regular classroom? Does the young mother give up child care benefits that are provided by the alternative school? If she does find day care somewhere else and she is able to attend the regular school, is she able to successfully complete the course work she is taking? If so, are the courses she is taking at the regular school worth the trade-off of added day care expense? Does the regular school offer the best employment and career options? Each teen parent will have different responses to these questions. The questions to ask are: Do school districts have the options in place to help meet the needs of the pregnant and parenting teens? Is there an attitude in the school systems that values mothers and their families for the contributions that they can make to the community, or are they seen as a drain on the community's assets?

Public Perception: Punishment vs. Special Treatment

Adolescent pregnancy and parenting may be viewed in some communities as a polarizing issue. Some groups want to punish pregnant and parenting teens for their "indiscretions" and make comments such as "It's their own fault they're pregnant. They are sexually active; they deserve it." Others see the fact that these pregnant and parenting teens are not married as a problem: "If only the girls would marry the fathers of their children. Where are the fathers?" Others find programs for pregnant teens an encouragement for other young women to have children.

On the other hand, some communities view pregnant and parenting teens as potentially positive contributors to the community. After all, their children represent the sum of the human capital of the next generation of citizens. The success of alternative programs for pregnant and parenting teens can be enhanced or diminished by the public perceptions surrounding them.

Work Force Preparedness vs. College Liberal Arts Preparedness

If the purpose of schooling is to prepare young people for the work force and eventual financial self-sufficiency, alternative schools for pregnant and parenting teens should be training young teen mothers in the skills needed to engage successfully in the job market, maintain a job, and develop the skills necessary for retraining as the job market changes over the next half century. It is a fact that people entering the job market today are expected to live longer and to be engaged in meaningful employment over a longer life span. How does this trend mesh with the purpose of alternative schools?

It is an interesting quirk of fate that early alternative schools in this country were originally started as places where employed youth could go to finish their education while maintaining a job (Kelly 1993). Over the years, the target of alternative education has shifted from employed youth unable to attend regular classes because of work obligations to maladjusted youth and, more recently, to educational experimentation. Emphasis on job skills has been an important part of many alternative education programs for pregnant and parenting teens and may often be associated with vocational education programs. There seems to be an assumption that pregnant and parenting teens should be tracked into vocational programs (many of which are supposed to result in immediate employment after high school graduation) rather than into college preparatory classes, even though participation in college preparatory classes presents a student with the most options for future employment.

Such tracking tends to play into the recent trends of stereotyping young single mothers as lazy, welfare-driven, uneducated young women who need to work at whatever job is available in order to get off the welfare rolls. Stereotyping teen parents not only does the teen parent and her family a disservice but also does a disservice to the general public by limiting the potential of many gifted women who could contribute in significant ways to the community.

If we stop stereotyping pregnant and parenting teens, it becomes clear that an array of options in education are necessary for pregnant and parenting teens to succeed. Some teen parents may want to complete a vocational track, others may be interested in completing college preparatory programs, and still others may want to complete high school through the GED programs available. School districts should be encouraged to offer an array of educational options (including regular and alternative education opportunities) to meet the varying needs of the students.

Chapter Twelve
A Comparison of the Models

In an effort to provide educational services for pregnant and parenting teens, various models of schools and school-related programs have emerged within local communities. The models examined in this chapter focus on the completion of a student's academic high school education. Programs for pregnant and parenting teens may offer other types of education, such as contraceptive, health, or nutritional. The sharing of information in these areas may or may not be conducted through schools. For organizational purposes, academic education that leads to the completion of high school is used as the point of comparison of these models.

After the five models for alternative education programs for pregnant and parenting teens (alternative school, cooperative school, community-based program, tutoring services, and in-school program) have been compared in the text and compared graphically in terms of school district involvement (figure 12.1) and implementation issues (table 12.1), matrixes of academic considerations for each type of program will be presented.

Definitions of Models
The five alternative education models are defined as follows.

1. *Alternative school.* This can be defined as an optional program leading to a high school diploma and designed to accommodate students who meet specific criteria. For example, alternative schools may be designed for students with poor reading ability, students with exceptional artistic talent, or, in this case, pregnant and parenting students. Once the pregnant and parenting students are identified, they attend a school that is within their district or school corpora-

Table 12.1 Implementation Issues

Issue	Alternative	Cooperative	Community	Tutoring	In-School
Location	Single site within a school district; building devoted to alternative and community-related programs, such as Head Start, job training, etc.	Centrally located site between school districts, often in a cooperative vocational school.	Basement of a church, hospital, or other community organization.	Home of the student.	Local school district.
Governance	School board of local school district.	By cooperative agreement between school districts.	Board of sponsoring organization.	Local school board policy.	Local school board.
Academics	Focus is on academics; completion of high school main focus.	Focus is on academics; completion of high school main focus.	Focus on goals of sponsoring group.	Completion of assignments.	Focus is on academics.
Child Care	On site or by referral.	On site or by referral.	On site or by referral.	In home of student during duration of tutoring.	May or may not be available depending on community.
Health Care	Nurse on site, and by agreement with other agencies.	Nurse on site.	Nurse may or may not be present.	Not immediately available as part of service.	Ranges from school nurse to school-based health clinic.
Transportation	Student and child must be transported.	Student and child must be transported.	Student and child must be transported.	Teacher needs transportation.	Students transported.

Funding	Through school board; may be supplemented through grants.	Participating districts' fee for services; grants.	From sponsoring agency.	Cost of tutor covered by school.	School funding.
Referrals	From single district.	From participating districts.	From sponsoring agency.	From classroom teachers; guidance office.	Depends on in-school programs offered.
Staffing Pattern	Staff representative of a variety of professions: educators, counselors, child care workers.	From a variety of professions: educators, counselors, child care workers.	From a variety of professions: educators, counselors, child care workers.	Single teacher.	School personnel.
Prepartum and Postpartum Attendance Regulations	Established by school district policy.	Each participating district establishes its own policy within general parameters of program.	Established by sponsoring agency.	Dependent on medical excuse.	Varies by school district.
Counseling Services	May be built into program.	May be built into program.	May be built into program.	Not available.	School counselors.
Administration	Principal of alternative school responsible to superintendent.	Director responsible to superintendent of co-op school.	Nonschool personnel.	Teacher responsible to principal and to other teachers she or he represents.	Principal of high school responsible to superintendent.

tion and that is specifically designed for them or, at least, to meet some of their needs. The local board of the school district is the governing body, and the school sometimes has additional contractual commitments from other funding sources. The AECYM is an example of an alternative school.

2. *Cooperative school.* Through a cooperative school, several school districts or corporations may arrange for jointly funded programs and services. In this model, once a pregnant or parenting young woman is identified, she leaves her school system and attends a special program designed to meet her specific needs. The governing board of the cooperative school is composed of representatives from the school boards of participating school districts.

3. *Community-based program.* This may be defined as a program operated by a community organization in conjunction with a local school district. This type of alternative education program may be housed in community or employment centers, churches, hospitals, etc. Although some funding may come from the local school district, the main funding for community-based programs comes through outside grants from organizations such as United Way, churches, foundations, hospitals, and government grants that are not school-related. When funding or in-kind contributions do come from a local school district, they may cover the cost of academic components such as books, educational materials, or teachers' salaries.

Community-based programs may be further divided into residential and nonresidential programs. Residential programs provide housing for pregnant and parenting teens in a group home setting, but students attend local school districts for academic instruction. Nonresidential community-based programs provide academic instruction at a community organization other than the local school district. The pregnant and parenting teens live away from the community-based site and travel to it instead of traveling to the local school district. Various combinations may exist; for example, a teen parent in a residential group home may attend an alternative academic program in a community setting.

4. *Tutoring services.* Some school districts provide tutoring services in the student's home during pregnancy and afterwards. The local school

board is the governing body responsible for this kind of program.

5. *In-school program.* Through an in-school program, pregnant and parenting teens remain in the school they were attending at the time of their pregnancy. Some schools have special classes for pregnant and parenting teens; others provide day care, health services through school clinics, and counseling services, while still other schools provide no additional services for their pregnant and parenting students. The local school board is the governing body.

In the following pages, these five models will be compared in terms of location, academics, child care, health, transportation, funding, referrals, staffing patterns, prenatal and postnatal attendance regulations, counseling services, and administration. Figure 12.1 shows a comparison of the models in terms of school district involvement, and table 12.1 gives a concise rendering of the comparisons in the text.

Implementation Issues
Location
Alternative

Alternative schools, located within the jurisdiction of a single school district, may be found in buildings devoted to alternative programs and community-related programs such as Head Start, job training, etc. The AECYM was housed in a school district building, which also housed the Head Start program. The site was within one mile of 60 percent of the participants.

Cooperative

Cooperative school programs may be located at the cooperative school campus or at one of the p`articipating school sites. In the cooperative school described in chapter 13, the alternative program for pregnant and parenting teens was housed at the cooperative school's vocational campus.

Community

Community programs are located at a site chosen by the sponsoring organization. For example, programs are housed in hospitals, churches, or community centers.

Alternative Program

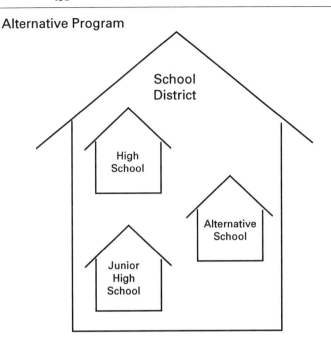

Cooperative School

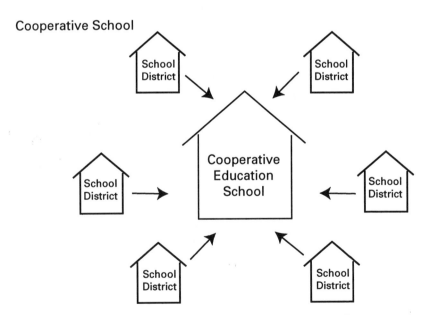

Figure 12.1. A Comparison of Models by School District Involvement

Community Program

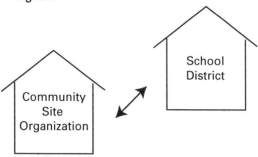

Home Tutoring

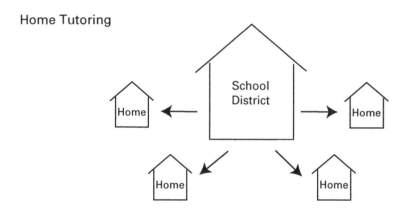

In-School Program

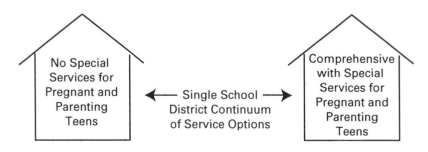

Tutoring
Tutoring programs take place in the home of the pregnant and/or parenting teen.

In-School
In-school programs are housed at the district high schools.

Governance
Alternative
Alternative schools are governed by the local school board. Some school policies established by the local school board allow students from other school districts to attend. However, the policies by which the alternative school operates are established by a single school board. There may be an additional advisory board or committee that oversees nonacademic components of the program, as was the case in part 2. However, the ultimate authority for the alternative school lies with the local school board.

Cooperative
Cooperative school programs exist through mutual agreement between school districts, with each participating district electing a representative to the cooperative school board. The cooperative school board, containing representatives from each participating district, oversees the operation of the cooperative school's program for pregnant and parenting teens. An advisory board may supplement the work of the school, but the ultimate authority for the operation of a cooperative program is the cooperative school board.

Community
Community programs are governed by the sponsoring agency's board of directors.

Tutoring
Tutoring programs are the responsibility of the local district's school board.

In-School
In-school programs are governed by local school boards.

Academics

Many programs provide a variety of services in addition to academic or educational training, but all programs can be differentiated by the hub around which they operate. For example, some schools have as their overall objective the development of well-rounded individuals who contribute to the well-being of society. With this as a goal, intellectual education and academic pursuits are placed within a more general context. Some programs have as their goal the self-sufficiency of the pregnant and parenting teen, and self-sufficiency is defined primarily as completion of high school. Much of the debate on school reform and on providing services to pregnant and parenting teens focuses on this issue of the school's responsibility for the nonacademic aspects of the students' lives.

Alternative

In alternative schools the main focus of the program is the attainment of a high school diploma. This can be achieved through instruction in the course work necessary for the accumulation of the Carnegie units needed for graduation, through participation in a basic education program designed to achieve the General Education Degree, or through vocational education programs.

Cooperative

Attainment of a high school diploma is the main focus of cooperative school programs. This is achieved through the Carnegie unit system, basic education programs, vocational education courses, or a combination of these.

Community

In community programs, the main focus is on nonacademic elements. Although academic instruction may be offered as a component of a program (through tutoring, classroom instruction, or other formats), a community-based program focuses on the goals and objectives of the sponsoring agency. For example, residential programs for pregnant and parenting·teens provide housing, food, and other services geared toward the general health and well-being of the mother and the child. Academics are considered in the overall scheme through arrangements with the local school district, tutoring, or other activities.

Tutoring

Through a tutoring program a student completes assignments prepared at the direction of the student's high school teachers and delivered to the students' home on a regular basis by the tutor. The focus of the program is on the completion of assignments for specific courses. The overall academic focus would parallel the school with which this program is affiliated.

In-School

Pregnant and parenting teens in in-school programs would be required to complete the same course work as the other students within the high school. Although additional services may be provided for the pregnant and parenting teens, the academic course work is not altered and the attainment of a high school diploma is the main focus of the program.[1]

Child Care

Even if educational programs for pregnant and parenting teens do not provide child care directly on site, the issue of child care is central to parenting teens completing their high school education. In comprehensive programs regardless of setting, child care may be provided either directly on site, through referral or voucher systems, through relatives, or through family day care providers. Difficulties arise if no child care arrangements are available within the community at large. The child care issue for parenting teens is tied into the larger issue of child care within the community; it should therefore be noted that the information provided here is simplified for discussion purposes.

Alternative

Alternative schools designed for pregnant and parenting teens are specifically created to take into consideration the needs of this particular population. If child care is not provided on site, arrangements are generally part of the referral plan.

Cooperative

Cooperative schools are similar to alternative schools in their child care arrangements. However, cooperative schools must deal with child care issues in multiple communities because several school districts may participate in one program for parenting teens. It is not unusual for parenting teens enrolled in a school district that does not have child care to transfer their place of residence to another district that does provide it. The opposite may also occur, as happened in the cooperative school program examined in chapter 13: One parenting teen in that program moved from a school district that allowed students who attended the cooperative school to remain enrolled in the program for up to two years after the birth of the child to a district that required students to return to their school of origin two weeks after the birth of the child. Sherri made arrangements to be dropped off in the morning and picked up every afternoon at her old residence so that she could continue attending the cooperative program. Even though she had actually moved to another school district, she never notified counselors in either district. For Sherri, the hassle of daily transportation between old and new residences on a daily basis was more desirable than making other arrangements for child care. Such convoluted thinking is not unusual for teens in normal circumstances. Given the complications involved in teen parenting and the lack of available child care in some communities, such behavior can be expected.

Community

Child care issues in community-based programs may in fact be the center around which other services are provided. For example, a church may provide child care services for parenting teens during the school day and tutoring, recreation, or parenting classes after school. Other ways in which community programs provide child care are through referrals or on site, as in the case of some residential or hospital programs.

Tutoring

Except during the actual tutoring sessions, child care is generally not a problem for the student who is tutored in her own home. In my informal discussions with tutors, their stories of tutoring a teen parent while she was breast-feeding or bottle-feeding a child were not unusual. However, the issue of child care may become problematic when the student must return to school. This is a crucial tie: it is precisely for child care reasons that many teen mothers drop out of school.

In-School

Child care in schools is not as unheard of as it once was. In-school programs vary from no special services for parenting teens to in-school day care centers, which may be connected (especially in vocational schools) to actual child care classes. When child care is not available to teen parents in school, referral systems to community day care options are essential. Once again, the child care issue for teen parents is connected to the larger community child care needs.

Health Care Issues

In the educational models described below, health care can be provided on site, through a referral system, through a combination of both methods, or not at all.

Alternative

At minimum, a school nurse is present or available (according to school district policy) as part of one of the school district programs. Additional health services may be made available because of the special nature of the program for pregnant and parenting teens. Special classes in prenatal care, birth and delivery, and infant health care are some examples of health classes offered in alternative schools for pregnant and parenting teens. These may be offered either on site or through referrals. Some alternative schools may have school-based health clinics or access to clinics on a regular basis.

Cooperative

Cooperative agreements between schools may also include a range of health services similar to the options available to the alternative schools. A difficulty arises in providing health services to pregnant and parenting teens in a cooperative setting because the students are from different communities and school districts. Difficulties within the referral system are compounded in the cooperative school setting because each participating school district may have a different community health care system.

Community

The health care component of a community program for pregnant and parenting teens depends on the goals of the sponsoring agency. If a hospital is the sponsoring agency, the health care component of the program will be the main focus of the program. On the other hand, if the focus of the community program is child care, health care may be provided through a referral system or may not be part of the program at all.

Tutoring

Completion of academic assignments is the main focus of tutoring programs; therefore, health care is not part of the program unless the home tutors choose to offer information on their own or unless a special health course is offered for all pregnant teens on home tutoring. A nurse is not available; the student's health care system is the one that she has designed for herself. Another option is to provide a visiting nurse through a referral arrangement with a public health or other health care system.

In-School

The health care component of an in-school program may range from the services of the school nurse to the availability of a school-based clinic.

Transportation Issues

Transportation can include school buses, personal cars, taxis, public transit, walking, and hitchhiking. Depending on the availability and cost of each of these options, pregnant and parenting teens decide whether to attend a program, keep an appointment, use day care, attend school, etc. Therefore, issues of transportation (including road conditions) are important in planning programs for pregnant and parenting teens.

Alternative

In an alternative school setting, the students can use existing school transportation. The issue of transporting infants along with the student needs to be clarified. Some alternative schools that have day care facilities on campus have made arrangements to allow infants and toddlers on the regular school bus, other programs provide special buses for pregnant and parenting teens and their children, and still others provide taxicabs or public transportation passes.

Cooperative

Transportation issues in cooperative school programs are more complicated because they need to be coordinated not just within one community but between several participating school districts. Students may first need to take a school bus to their own school district and then transfer to a school bus that transports them to the cooperative school campus. This may result in several hours a day spent on a bus, and this can be physically challenging for a pregnant young woman. Transporting infants and toddlers between various school districts can also prove challenging when each school district has its own transportation policy. In addition, public transportation may or may not be available depending on the district. Providing transportation to cooperative school programs may require creative planning, including vouchers, transit passes, or funds for gas.

Community

The issues of transportation in community-based programs may be similar to those for alternative school programs in that they generally deal with a single community. However, transportation to a community-based program may be more difficult to provide because school transportation may not be readily available for other than school-related purposes. Community programs must rely heavily on the availability of public transportation or the use of personal vehicles; therefore, vouchers, transit passes, and funds for gas may be particularly useful.

Tutoring

In tutoring situations, transportation is not the issue for the students, but the tutor needs transportation to the student's home. Some transportation factors that need to be considered when planning tutoring programs include the distance between the school and students' homes, the distances between students' homes, road conditions, weather conditions, accessibility to school-owned vehicles, reimbursement for mileage when personal cars are used, the ease with which students' homes can be reached, and procedures to use in case of emergencies during travel.

Another transportation issue concerns the student's transportation to other than academic services. Pregnant and parenting teens and their children still require transportation to health, counseling, and other services that, in comprehensive programs, are readily accessible on site. In tutoring programs, the student must rely heavily on personal transportation arrangements. Making such arrangements can prove complicated and may appear insurmountable. If transportation is not part of the overall service plan for pregnant and parenting teens, then students should at least be counseled on how to make transportation arrangements. Lists of taxicab phone numbers, public transportation schedules, vouchers for gas, transit passes, and safety brochures for walking can be provided as resources for the pregnant and parenting teen who is part of a tutoring program.

In-School

Programs provided in the student's usual school district may involve the least complicated transportation issues. Given the usual school district transportation issues of scheduling, funding, and safety, the transportation of pregnant and parenting students and their children may add to these challenges. The same strategies used in alternative and cooperative schools may prove useful.

Funding Issues

Alternative

Funding for an alternative school may come directly from the school district, foundations, government grants, fees for service, or a combination of these. (This is discussed in greater detail in chapter 3.)

Cooperative

Funding for cooperative school programs comes from the participating school districts in a fee-for-service arrangement. (See chapter 13 for a more detailed discussion.) In addition, program funding may be supplemented through government grants or private foundations.

Community
A community program relies on the sponsoring agency for funds. The sponsoring agency may secure funds as a not-for-profit organization through fund-raising efforts, grants from foundations, government-sponsored programs, fees for services, the operating budget of the sponsoring agency, or a combination of sources.

Tutoring
Tutoring costs include the salary and travel expenses for the itinerant teacher who travels from one student's home to another. These funds come from the school district's budget and may be supplemented by funds from grants.

In-School
In-school programs are funded by the school district. Programs for pregnant and parenting teens may receive additional funds through grants.

Referral Issues
Referral systems are an integral part of service delivery to pregnant and parenting teens. No matter how good the services may be, they are of no use if a student cannot access the system. Referral systems can enhance the availability and use of a program, but several issues need to be resolved when one is established. First, the initial referral to the system (whether through the client herself, the client's parents, or a professional) is crucial. If initial referrals are successful, publicity and marketing issues and quality of service become important. Clients will tell other clients about the quality of the service. Potential clients may hear about a program through newspapers, radio, television, billboards, displays at malls, or shopping areas, etc. Second, once clients access a service delivery system, referrals to the full range of services can be achieved in several ways. The success of the formal linkages between the agencies providing the various services is vital. Referral protocols are established by mutual agreement

between agencies. In some service-delivery systems, direct providers have an informal, personal network whereby clients are referred from one service to another. In any referral system the issue of confidentiality must be addressed. Release-of-information forms need to be signed before information is shared with other agencies, before clients can be encouraged to make their own appointments with other providers, or before the service provider can make referrals in the presence of their clients. Issues of confidentiality can complicate a referral system if they are not properly addressed.

Alternative

Referrals to an alternative school within a given school district are made through the protocols established by the school district. Self-referrals and referrals through the guidance office, principal, or classroom teachers are all possible initiators of the referral system. In addition, because alternative schools are generally based on a wide range of services, referral systems often include a formal network of service delivery. Access to one service, the alternative school, provides access to other services such as child care, health care, or job training.

Cooperative

In a cooperative school program for pregnant and parenting teens, referrals come from the participating school districts. Referrals to other services are made either through self-referral or through provider contacts among the organizations that provide them. The referral system may be based on formal linkage agreements or on informal networking between the service providers working with pregnant and parenting teens in the community.

Community

Referrals to community-sponsored programs for pregnant and parenting teens may come from direct-service providers in other organizations, through self-referral, or through clients who have come to the sponsoring agency for other services. For example, in a hospital-sponsored program a teenager may be part of the adolescent clinic on an ongoing basis for regular health services. Enrollment in a teenage pregnancy program may come as part of these ongoing services.

Referrals to other services may be through self-referral, formal linkage agreements with other agencies, or informal networking among
direct-service providers working at the various agencies in the community.

Tutoring

Referrals for home tutoring are made by the classroom teacher, guidance officer, or school nurse and are made at the request of the parents and based on a medical excuse. Referrals for other services such
as child and health care are limited and may not be provided as part
of the tutoring program.

In-School

All children within the jurisdiction of the school district must attend school. Attendance at programs for pregnant and parenting
teens within a given school district is based on criteria established by
the school district and follows the district's general protocols. Referrals may come from the guidance office, a classroom teacher, a parent, or the principal.

Staffing and Personnel Issues

Staffing patterns in programs for pregnant and parenting teens can
be as simple as hiring an itinerant teacher for a tutoring program or
as complex as hiring a large staff with member service providers from
a variety of professions or linking service providers from a variety of
agencies.

Alternative

In alternative schools, several teachers may be needed to cover the
variety of courses offered at the school. In addition, an administrator, counselors, clerical personnel, health care workers, transportation personnel, and other employees are needed for the daily operation of the program. Whether these professionals are hired
solely for the alternative school, shared among other programs, or
linked through outside agencies depends on such factors as the size
of the program, the number of linkages with other agencies, and
the availability of funds. Alternative schools for pregnant and
parenting teens may have formal linkages to other agencies in or-

der to provide additional services such as health care, in-depth counseling, and transportation. If this is the case, an understanding regarding the training needs of the personnel at those agencies needs to be formed. Issues such as joint orientation and training opportunities, supervision of employees, and scheduling should be considered.

Cooperative

In a cooperative school, the staffing patterns may be similar to those in an alternative school. However, because the cooperative school deals with youth from several school districts, the coordination of staff may be more complex.

Community

In a community-sponsored program, the main group of professionals hired by the sponsoring agency may not be teachers. Depending on the focus of the sponsoring agency, the staffing patterns may be more similar to those in a medical or a community agency model, in which case the educators may be considered adjunct members of the staff hired through cooperative agreements with outside agencies. The same issues (staff orientation and training, supervision of employees, scheduling, etc.) that are part of the alternative and cooperative programs require attention during the planning and operation of a community program.

Tutoring

In a tutoring program staffing changes are at a minimum. The addition of an itinerant teacher is all that is required. In-service training on the implementation of the tutoring program could assist both the itinerant teacher and the classroom teachers.

In-School

Depending on the extent of the program offered by a school district, staffing patterns may range from little or no change in the existing staff to the hiring of staff for new instructional or service units within the district. The issues of staff orientation, supervision, coordination, etc., are similar to those for the other types of programs.

Prenatal and Postnatal Attendance Regulations and Issues

Regulations regarding attendance at programs for pregnant and parenting teens vary greatly depending on the focus of the program and the criteria for participation in it.

Alternative

In alternative schools, attendance at programs for pregnant and parenting teens may begin as soon as the student confirms her pregnancy with a doctor's statement. Other alternative schools may have quarterly or semester enrollment times. The postnatal stay may be as long as it takes to graduate from high school, particularly in schools that offer day care facilities for the children of students.

Cooperative

Attendance policies for cooperative school programs may create confusion among students from the various districts. For example, to continue attending a program and by using her own transportation arrangements, a student may choose not to report residential moves from one district with a liberal attendance policy to another with a limited attendance policy, or she may move from a school district with a limited attendance policy into a school district with a liberal attendance policy.

Community

Attendance at community programs is based on the focus of the program. For example, a hospital-sponsored program may provide services for the pregnant teenager as soon as pregnancy is confirmed. Attendance may continue for weeks or even years after the child is born. A residential program may allow youth to stay in it for several years depending on the policies established by the sponsoring agency.

Tutoring

Enrollment in a tutoring program requires a medical condition that is verified by a doctor's statement. Parenting teens are required to return to school based on the doctor's recommendation.

In-School

Attendance at in-school programs depends on the services offered in the school district. Attendance policies may vary from no special policy for pregnant and parenting teens to special arrangements that allow legitimate absences for doctor's appointments and for sick days for the teen's child, as well as for the teen herself.

Counseling Services and Issues
When counseling services are provided, issues such as confidentiality, the type of counseling, the amount of space for counseling services, and transportation need to be considered.

Alternative
Counseling services are often an integral part of alternative schools. In-depth counseling may be available through referral systems established through formal or informal linkages with other organizations and agencies.

Cooperative
Educational counseling services are generally available through the school counseling office. Additional counseling services may be available through formal or informal linkages with other organizations.

Community
Depending on the focus of the community-based program, counseling may or may not be available. In community-based programs, counseling may be the core around which additional services are arranged.

Tutoring
Other than educational counseling available through the school guidance office, counseling is generally not available to students who are tutored at home.

In-School
In-school programs offer pregnant and parenting students at least the same amount of counseling that is available to all students within the school district. Special arrangements may exist for additional counseling services, particularly in school districts that have school-based health clinics.

Administration Issues

Alternative

The principal is responsible for the day-to-day operation of the school and generally reports to the superintendent of the school district.

Cooperative

The administrator/head teacher often reports to the superintendent of the cooperative school.

Community

Nonschool personnel may be responsible for the day-to-day operation of the program. They often report to the board of directors of the sponsoring organization.

Tutoring

The individual teacher is responsible to the school principal and to the other teachers whom he or she represents when the teacher visits students in their homes.

In-School

The principal of the school is responsible for in-school programs and reports to the superintendent of schools.

Matrixes of Academic Considerations for Each Type of Program

The following matrixes further delineate the differences in academic considerations among the five models of alternative education programs for pregnant and parenting teens. These matrixes interact in complex ways and to varying degrees. Each matrix is accompanied by a table, which provides a graphic depiction of the interacting elements. These matrixes are meant to be starting points for discussion and are neither comprehensive nor mutually exclusive.

Alternative School

A graphic representation of this matrix is shown in table 12.2.

Student Issues

To attend an alternative school, a student must meet the criteria for attendance established by the local school board. The criteria may include poor academic performance, pregnancy, or a poor attendance record. Pregnant and parenting teens may already be attending an alternative school for other than pregnancy-related reasons. However, this discussion focuses on alternative schools designed specifically for pregnant and parenting teens.

Curriculum Issues

Student. If a student transfers from a regular to an alternative school for pregnant and parenting teens, she may need to drop or add courses based on the alternative school courses. There may be courses specifically designed for pregnant teens such as Health During Pregnancy or Child Care.

Curriculum. Alternative schools offer a variety of curricular options. Some schools focus on completion of high school through Carnegie unit courses; others focus on completion of the General Education Diploma (GED); still others offer vocational training opportunities. Some alternative schools offer a combination of options.

Instructional Materials, Methods, and Issues

Student. The instructional materials and methods used will depend on the courses the student decides to take at the alternative school.

Curriculum. Because the alternative school is designed to meet the needs of a specific population, the instructional materials and methods are designed to meet specific curricular needs. For example, parenting teens may receive credit for working in the child care center that their child attends.

Instructional Materials and Methods. The instructional materials and methods vary and are based on the goals and objectives of the alternative program.

Environmental Issues

Student. In an alternative school the student has the opportunity to interact with other students.

Table 12.2 Alternative School Matrix

	Student	Curriculum	Instructional Materials and Methods	Environment	Educator
Student	Students must meet criteria established for alternative program.				
Curriculum	Students may need to drop or add courses based on purpose of alternative school.	Carnegie units, preparation for GED, vocational special courses based on criteria for attendance.			
Instructional Materials and Methods	Dependent on goals and objectives of alternative program.	Additional courses and materials based on special need of student, child care, parenting, etc.	Varied, depending on goals and objectives of alternative program.		
Environment	Interaction with other students.	May be enhanced by more facilities and availability of labs.	Group instruction and possible projects; possible addition to other methods; wide variety.	Room arrangement and facilities designed for pregnant women: access to rest rooms; chairs/tables.	
Educator	Able to focus on students because of the criteria for attendance.	May need additional training in area of special need of student.	May need additional training based on spcial needs of student.	Environment different from regular classroom; faculty may feel sense of isolation from other faculty, staff; number of colleagues limited at site.	No special certification for teaching at an alternative school.

Curriculum. The more specialized equipment and other facilities are available, the more the curriculum is enhanced.

Instructional Materials and Methods. A wide variety of instructional materials and methods (such as group work, projects, and skills training on special equipment) are available. The instructional materials and methods are dependent on the goals and objectives of the alternative school. Since some alternative schools are designed for youth who generally are not succeeding in the traditional classroom, instructional methods may focus on experiential learning techniques and other activity-oriented methods.

Environment. In an alternative school designed for pregnant and parenting teens, the furniture may be more accessible to pregnant women. Chairs and tables may be used instead of school desks with immovable seats and arms. Access to rest room facilities, a limited number of stairs, or the availability of an elevator may enhance the learning experience of a pregnant or parenting teen.

Educator-Related Issues

Student. In an alternative school, the educator is able to focus on the special needs of the student, because the criteria for attendance determine the school's design.

Curriculum. The educator may need additional training in areas outside his or her area of certification.

Instructional Materials and Methods. Additional training in instructional methods most suited for the alternative school population may enhance the teacher's ability to meet their needs.

Environment. Working in an alternative setting may be challenging for some teachers. The environment is different from that at a traditional school campus. The teaching staff at alternative schools may be small, and the teachers work with many staff members from other professions such as counseling, health care, and social work. This

Table 12.3 Cooperative School Matrix

	Student	Curriculum	Instructional Materials and Methods	Environment	Educator
Student	Student must meet criteria for participation; each participating school district may have differing criteria.				
Curriculum	Student may have to drop or add classes based on availability; balance with other districts.	Based on Carnegie units; balance between participating schools; additional offerings at site (vocational, GED); designed for pregnancy.			
Instructional Materials and Methods	Student exposed to methods and materials from different schools.	Need to balance the materials from different school districts.	A variety of methods, including individual and group instruction.		
Environment	Campus setting; interaction among students with similar conditions and students attending different programs.	Additional offerings at site (vocational, GED).	Designed for pregnancy; facilities may be enhanced.	Located away from school of origin; additional transportation may be required.	
Educator	Interaction with new teachers; smaller class size.	Must balance requirements from each participating school district.	Organizes incoming and outgoing materials of each subject teacher in school of origin.	Must deal with transportation of students, time on bus, the variety of students.	Works on campus, may need special training.

interprofessional environment requires different skills from those needed by an educator in a standard school, where most of the staff are educators and there are only a limited number of counselors and other professionals.

Educator. At present there is no special certification for teaching in an alternative school.

Cooperative School
A graphic representation of this matrix is shown in table 12.3.

Student Issues
The pregnant and parenting teenagers who attend a cooperative school program must meet the criteria established by their local school district within the general guidelines established by the cooperative school board. Each participating district may have differing criteria for attendance. For example, a particular district may allow a student to be sent to the cooperative school as soon as pregnancy is confirmed and will allow the student to stay until the completion of high school. However, a participating school in another district may decide to send only pregnant students in their third trimester, and the student must return to the participating school two weeks after the birth of the child.

Curriculum Issues
Student. The student may have to drop or add courses based on the type of the courses offered at the cooperative school program. Depending on the number of participating school districts, the list of course offerings may have to be limited.

Curriculum. The curriculum may be based on Carnegie units of study, GED basic subjects, vocational training opportunities, or the specific needs of pregnant and parenting teens.

Instructional Materials, Methods, and Issues
Student. The students who attend a cooperative school program are exposed to students from other school districts. Learning about different school districts and course materials provides young mothers

with an opportunity to expand their realm of experience.

Curriculum. The curriculum materials from the various participating school districts need to be balanced. For example, three students may be enrolled to take geometry, but each school district may have a different content sequence, use a different textbook, and have different grading policies.

Instructional Materials and Methods. A variety of instructional methods (including individual and group instruction, hands-on vocational training, and experimental learning activities such as the day care center) can be used in the cooperative program.

Environmental Issues

Student. The students who attend a program at the cooperative school campus have an opportunity not only to meet students from other districts but also to meet other pregnant and parenting teens who may be experiencing similar problems and concerns.

Curriculum. Since the cooperative school's program is generally held on campus, the pregnant and parenting students have an opportunity to take advantage of other courses (for example, vocational, computer, or advanced academic) offered at the site.

Instructional Materials and Methods. Since the cooperative school's program is specifically designed for pregnant and parenting teens, their needs can be taken into consideration when instructional activities are planned. Stairs, rest room facilities, and table and chair arrangements can all be modified, to create a comfortable environment for learning.

Environment. Additional transportation for students and their infants may need to be considered, since the cooperative school may be located far away from the school of origin.

Educator-Related Issues

Student. The students have an opportunity to meet new teachers and to be taught in smaller classes with other students who have similar concerns and issues related to pregnancy and parenting.

Curriculum. The educator must balance the number of students, the number of courses that each student takes, and the requirements of each participating school district. Time is required to develop a common core curriculum that fulfills these requirements.

Instructional Materials and Methods. The educator must organize the incoming and outgoing assignments and instructional materials of each of the participating school districts and of the applicable teachers within each district.

Environment. Transportation of students to and from the cooperative school campus may be a problem for the educator. Educators may need to deal with pregnant and parenting students who have to spend two or three hours a day riding buses.

Educator. The educators teach on the cooperative school's campus. Since they work with pregnant and parenting teens, educators may require additional training in the special needs and characteristics of this group.

Community School
A graphic representation of this matrix is shown in table 12.4.

Student Issues
Students who attend a community program are identified by criteria established by the sponsoring organization. For example, obstetric patients at a hospital may be entitled to attend the academic program sponsored by that hospital.

Curriculum Issues
Student. The student may need to drop or add courses based on arrangements made between the local school district and the sponsoring agency.

Curriculum. The educational package of a community-based program may focus on specific topics other than academics. For ex-

Table 12.4 Community School Matrix

	Student	Curriculum	Instructional Materials and Methods	Environment	Educator
Student	Students identified by attendance at community center, hospital, church.				
Curriculum	Student continues attendance and course work at original school.	Educational package may focus on a special topic of the sponsoring agency.			
Instructional Materials and Methods	Based on immediate need of client.	Based on professional training methods of sponsoring organization.	Based on an interplay of factors.		
Environment	Transportation to site may be difficult.	Academic component may be provided on site or at local school.	Usually located at sponsoring organization; availability may be affected by the type of site.	Community facility is the hub of the community program.	
Educator	Interacts with student in nonteacher-student model or professional-client model.	Delivers information through the professional model of sponsoring agency.	May not be trained in pedagogy.	Environment may inhibit educator's ability to work one-on-one.	May be trained in other than education (e.g., sociology, medicine, counseling).

ample, a program sponsored through a hospital may have special classes on prenatal care, delivery, or child care, and the student may not receive academic credit for them. A program sponsored by a church group may provide academic tutoring for the pregnant and parenting student during afterschool hours. Young women in a residential program may attend the local high school but may have special recreational and counseling opportunities. Outreach activities for those enrolled in the local school but not enrolled in the residential setting may also be provided.

Instructional Materials, Methods, and Issues

Student. Instructional materials need to present information about pregnancy and parenting at a junior-high readability and interest level. If the student has special needs, the materials may need to address those needs. For example, a student with severe reading problems may need to have medical information about prescriptions written out in very simple language and verbally explained.

Curriculum. The curriculum may reflect the professional training methods of the organization sponsoring the program. A program sponsored by a hospital may provide a curriculum prepared for nurses to use with pregnant and parenting teens in one-on-one counseling, whereas a residential program may bring in outside speakers for group discussions.

Instructional Materials and Methods. The instructional materials and methods in community-based programs are based on the dynamic interplay of, among other things, the focus of the sponsoring agency, the amount of funding for materials and personnel, time, and the needs of the student. Except for the focus of the sponsoring agency, these same factors influence any curriculum in general. Only in community programs does the focus of the sponsoring agency have an affect on the instruction of the pregnant and parenting teens.

Environmental Issues

Student. Since community-based programs are usually housed away from the school, transportation for the students may be a problem.

Location, accessibility, and safety are key factors in student attendance at the program.

Curriculum. If the academic component is at the local school and the rest of the program is off that school's campus, transportation between the two sites may influence the time a student devotes to academic activities.

Instructional Materials and Methods. The location of the program can enhance the instructional materials and methods used. For example, in a hospital, procedures using lab equipment can be demonstrated and experimental learning techniques can be used. On the other hand, an afterschool tutoring program at the local community center may only have access to books and paper.

Environment. In community-based programs the community organization is the hub around which other activities operate. Therefore, issues of location and accessibility play an important part in the program's success.

Educator-Related Issues

Student. The "educator" in a community-based program may not actually be trained as one. Therefore, the educator-student relationship may be one of professional-client, volunteer-individual, or peer helping peer.

Curriculum. The educator delivers the information in the curriculum through the professional model of the sponsoring agency. For example, in a hospital program a social worker may provide prescription information to a teen mom on a one-to-one basis rather than hold an instructional class on how to read prescriptions for all students involved in the program.

Instructional Materials and Methods. The instructors may come from a variety of professions and may therefore not be trained in pedagogy.

Environment. The location of the community-based program may detract from the educator's ability to work with the students in both one-on-one and group activities. For example, one-on-one tutoring in a church basement may not allow for privacy, although it may provide an opportunity for teen mothers to socialize with one another. The educator's transportation to the site and his or her safety, as well as the students' safety at the site, are important considerations in community-based programs.

Educator. The staff working with the pregnant and parenting teenagers may come from a variety of professions other than education, or may have no professional training at all. Care must be taken to provide staff with the necessary orientation to work with pregnant and parenting teens and to provide information on working with other staff members, who may have varying professional models by which they operate. For example, the medical procedures in which nurses and doctors are trained are very different from the social work model for providing service, which is very different from volunteers' models for service. An understanding of these differences is extremely important for school personnel who are involved in providing linkages between the school district and the community-based program.

Home Tutoring
During tutoring a teacher visits a student in the student's home on a regular basis. The number of instructional contact hours per week is determined by state law. (See also table 12.5.)

Student Issues
The pregnant student is labeled as a child who has a medical problem and is under doctor's care. Tutoring begins at the discretion of the doctor and continues as long as the doctor allows. A medical release is generally required for the student to return to school.

Curriculum Issues
Student. The student may continue in the courses she was taking at the time of her pregnancy.

Curriculum. The courses the student is carrying are based on the Carnegie system of educational units required for graduation.

Table 12.5 Home Tutoring Matrix

	Student	Curriculum	Instructional Materials and Methods	Environment	Educator
Student	Student is labeled as having medical problem.				
Curriculum	Student continues in same courses.	Based on Carnegie units needed for graduating.			
Instructional Materials and Methods	Student must complete assignments somewhat independently of instruction.	Courses may be dropped because of lack of materials, accessibility of labs.	Book work; projects; limited discussion.		
Environment	Student remains in her own home; little interaction with peers; tremendous isolation in rural areas.	Teachers must carry all equipment, materials.	Limited to activities that can be completed at home.	Ranges from single student at home to whole families; room for instruction limited.	
Educator	Educator must contact students to set up appointments; phone tag; limited phone access.	Amount of preparation for each student times the number of students.	One-on-one relationship with student.	Safety to be considered; number of students visited depends on location.	Educator must be generalist; course work over junior/senior high school level.

Instructional Materials, Methods, and Issues
Student. The student must complete a series of assignments conveyed by the home tutor from the instructor at the school.

Curriculum. The student may have to drop courses for a number of reasons, such as lack of portable equipment needed for completion of assignment or lack of qualified tutors in high-level mathematics or science.

Instructional Materials and Methods. Assignments are such that a student has to read large amounts of information from textbooks. The tutoring session may be confined to reviewing previous assignments and assigning the next set of assignments. The amount of discussion is limited and depends on the time available and the number of courses carried by the student.

Environmental Issues
Student. The student remains in her own home, and this may lead to a sense of isolation, and to limited opportunities to interact with peers.

Curriculum. The teacher is required to carry all the materials for all the subjects of each student from house to house. Therefore, the number of courses taken may be limited by what the tutor can transport.

Instructional Materials and Methods. Assignments are limited to the types of activities that a student can do on her own, in a home setting, and with limited access to outside resources such as a library or computer.

Environment. Home tutoring takes place in the home of the student. Students come from all backgrounds, and the home environment may or not not be conducive to study and may range from a clean, neat house, where the student is waiting at the kitchen table to a hostile environment, where the family dog is chained on the front porch and guards the only entrance to the home.

Educator-Related Issues
Student. Home tutoring requires that the student and the tutor re-

main in contact even on days when the tutor is not scheduled to visit. Changes in either the student's or the tutor's schedule may result in time spent on phone calls, time spent on visits to students' homes when they are not there, and students waiting for tutors who do not arrive. This is especially difficult if a student does not have phone service.

Curriculum. Each student generally carries more than one course. Therefore, the tutor has an overwhelming amount of preparation work. The amount of preparation is equal to the number of students the tutor visits multiplied by the number of subjects each student carries.

Instructional Materials and Methods. A home tutoring situation may allow a tutor to develop a one-on-one relationship with the student, so that the student gets individual help in subjects that are difficult. The amount of help the student receives depends on the expertise of the tutor.

Environment. The safety of the tutor and the student during home visits is an important point to consider in program planning. Tutors may be required to visit dangerous or unfamiliar areas and to travel to opposite ends of the geographical boundaries of the school district. Travel time, road conditions, and weather are a few conditions that affect the educator's ability to deliver services to the student. Students are asked to receive a stranger into their home on a regular basis.

Educator. In order to teach a variety of subjects to students with varying ability and at various grade levels, the tutor must be a generalist.

In-School Programs
In-school programs vary greatly and are not described here.

Note

1. Since alternative schools are sometimes criticized for lacking college-prep course work, a tutoring or in-school program might be a better option for a college-bound teen, since college-prep work would be included as part of the regular high school curriculum.

Chapter Thirteen
A Portrait from Practice

The importance of educational options for pregnant and parenting teens cannot be overemphasized. In part 2 I described the results of my research project, conducted in the spring of 1990. In chapter 12 I made a comparison of the five educational models based on formal and informal interviews with both administrators and direct-service providers who focus their efforts on issues facing pregnant and parenting teens. The focus in this chapter now turns from research to practice.

From 1979 to 1988 I was the coordinator of an alternative education program for pregnant and parenting teens at a cooperative school. The information presented here is based on those nine years of experience plus my experience as president of a statewide professional council on adolescent pregnancy and parenting.

The term *cooperative school model* means a program to which more than one school corporation or district sends its students (see chapter 12). The term *cooperative* does not refer to the instructional technique of cooperative learning, although some cooperative schools do incorporate cooperative learning methods of instruction. A cooperative school operates by cooperative agreements between school districts, provides vocational, special education, purchasing, library, and other resources that one school corporation alone could not afford.

Services for pregnant and parenting adolescents can be expensive. Therefore several school districts may get together to provide them either through existing agreements, by adding the program for pregnant and parenting teens to a list of other programs offered by an existing cooperative school, or through the creation of a new agreement, which results in cooperative services between school districts where no shared services existed before.

Education programs for pregnant and parenting teens developed through existing cooperative agreements (in which other services such as vocational training, purchasing, and curriculum resources are already shared) are usually located at the cooperative school campus that houses the other jointly purchased services. Cost sharing allows school districts that are strapped for funds to provide services that would be too costly to provide for only a handful of students.

Access

Students from participating school districts attend this type of program through the financial support of their local school district. A fee for services is generally charged. Each school district pays a set amount for a student to attend the program.

This fee can be paid in a number of ways. Some cooperatives operate on a yearly basis. A participating school district pays a set fee to send as many students as it chooses. For example, assume the cost of operating the program is $100,000 (mostly in teacher salaries). If ten school districts participate, each district pays $10,000. During the school year, when a student becomes pregnant and chooses to attend the teenage pregnancy and parenting program offered at the cooperative school, the school district has already bought into the program and the student may attend. This approach could be viewed as an insurance policy. Based on statistics from previous years, a school district could anticipate an approximate number of pregnant and parenting teens in a given year. This method of payment divides the cost of the program equally among participating districts, even though the districts do not send the same number of students. This may appear unfair to the districts that only have one or two pregnant students in a given year while other districts may have ten or fifteen. Although this approach may at first appear to benefit the cooperative school, since the participating districts are purchasing services that they may not use, it can be difficult for the cooperative school if the actual number of students is greater than the anticipated number.

Another approach to financing is the fee-for-service approach whereby the participating school districts pay for only the exact number of students that they send to the cooperative school program. It may be beneficial for the participating school district to pay at the end of the school year, once there is a definite count of the number of students using the service. The difficulty in programming for pregnant and parenting teenagers is determining the number of them who will need a service in a given year. If the participating school districts wait until the end of the school year to pay for the service, the cooperative school must operate the service with its own funds until the books are reconciled at the end of the year. Even if the numbers of participants are projected from previous years and the school districts provide funds at the beginning of the school year for the operation of the program and then reconcile the actual costs at the end of the year, the cooperative school must decide its staffing patterns and other budgetary considerations at the beginning of the school year.

A third option for payment is based on quarterly attendance or some other divided payment (monthly, weekly). Because teenagers do not get pregnant on a defined schedule, students in pregnant and parenting alternative education programs enter and exit programs at various times during a given school year. How the cooperative school and the participating school districts resolve the issues of payment determines the issues of attendance and participation. By manipulation of the attendance and payment policies, a school district may say it participates in and provides service for pregnant and parenting teenagers, but in reality, attendance and payment policies provide subtle (and sometimes not so subtle) pressure on pregnant and parenting teens either to leave the cooperative school program and return to regular classes at the participating district's school, to have home tutoring instead of continuing in the cooperative school, to remain in the cooperative school instead of returning to classes in the regular school district, or to drop out altogether if their school district only participates in the cooperative program for students who are pregnant and does not provide services for parenting students.

All of these variations exemplify the complex relation between funding policies, attendance, and participation in these programs.

Program Components

In the cooperative school described here, three general services were offered: education (academic and vocational), child care, and counseling. Additional services such as food subsidies, health care, and in-depth counseling were provided through referral.

Academics

In the cooperative system, providing an academic program that resulted in a high school diploma was challenging and complicated. If the students came from various school districts, courses with the same title might have different textbooks, central concepts, requirements, assignments, and tests. Since the cooperative school offered academic credit in the form of Carnegie units, a decision had to be made whether to use the assignments, textbooks, and requirements expected of the student's school district or whether to design one common course for use by the cooperative program.

Initially, the former course was chosen and what resulted was an individualized curriculum, in which each student was essentially completing assignments from her local school district. This allowed each student to enter the cooperative alternative educational system as she became pregnant and to return to her local school district at any time after her delivery. In this way the participating students kept up with their local school district assignments. However, this approach was time-consuming and became an organizational nightmare. For example, assume that one student from each grade level (7–12) was sent by each of the participating local schools and that each student was taking from three to five courses; this leads to over 100 different courses taught by each teacher in a given year. The staffing hours needed to teach each student's courses varied based on the number of students attending the program, and placed the teachers in a precarious employment position, which was dependent on a fluctuating enrollment. Another concern was the logistics of gathering information from each local school district teacher who had the pregnant or parenting student in a class. This meant that some form of regular communication system had to exist between the students' teachers in the local school district and the teachers in the cooperative program. In addition to preparing materials for the student, the teacher in the local district would have to spend time conveying this information to the teacher in the cooperative school. In addition to teaching the individual subjects to each student, the teacher at the cooperative school would have to spend time reading each textbook, preparing different materials, and interacting with the local school teacher. (Copies of the paperwork trail created for this communication system, which can also be used in tutoring programs, can be found in appendix I.)

As the number of students increased in the cooperative school program, a new system had to be found to accommodate the students' academic needs. It was decided that core courses would be offered instead for all students who attended the cooperative program. However, another set of problems arose. This approach reduced the number of courses that a given teacher had to teach, but it required additional time for the teacher to prepare core courses and new course materials to meet the needs of students coming from various local school systems. In addition, this approach created a problem for the student who attended the cooperative program for only a short time during and after her pregnancy and then returned to her local school district for part of the school year, because common topics were addressed in varying sequence at the local school district. When a student returned to the local school district, she may have already covered the topic being discussed or may have missed other topics not covered.

Both these alternatives created certain trade-offs for the students. For example, some of the participating local districts decided to alleviate the confusion of conflicting course requirements by requiring the enrolled student of the cooperative program to stay in the program until the end of the school year. This may have been seen by some students as a way of "getting those pregnant girls out of the local school system"; on the other hand, it can be viewed as a way of ensuring that a student completed her course work for a given year in an atmosphere that was conducive to her special needs. Other participating school districts limited the time a young woman could be enrolled in the program by requiring enrollment to begin during the third trimester of pregnancy and to end two weeks after the birth of the child.

To resolve the academic issues involved in providing academic courses that result in Carnegie units of credit, some cooperative programs decided to provide the necessary preparation for passing the general equivalency diploma (GED) exam instead of regular academic classes. Trade-offs can be seen at work here also. By choosing this option, a pregnant and parenting student limits her future options for additional education and employment, but it can be seen as a way for youth who might otherwise drop out to complete high school.

As with any trade-off, problems arise. Ideally it is the responsibility of the school system to provide enough options so that each student can choose the best one for her individual circumstances, but the real world consists of limited funding, staff shortages, and various levels of student motivation. Trade-offs need not be permanent but are often necessary as programs develop and evolve to meet changing student needs. See figure 13.1 for the program of courses and activities at the cooperative school examined here.

Child Care

In the cooperative alternative education program for pregnant and parenting teenagers described in this study, the child care program changed between 1979 and 1988. During the first three years of the program, no child care was provided. Students who attended the program during their pregnancy were required to return to their local school district immediately afterward. Their child care arrangements were then the same as those of an adult mother and included:

- In-home care provided by the student's parent or other relative in the home of the student
- In-home care at someone else's home
- Dropping out of school to care for the child

No infant care programs were available in the community. Therefore, efforts to keep young women in school during their pregnancies were eventually thwarted because of lack of infant care.

As the realization grew that efforts to provide young mothers with an education were limited by the lack of available infant day care, it became apparent that day care options needed to be provided in the community. As a result, the students were allowed to

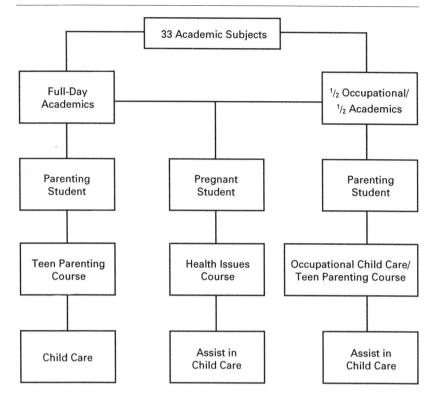

Figure 13.1. Student Course Strands and Activities Offered by the Cooperative School

Activities		
Name	**Type**	**Frequency**
Teen woman's self-awareness	Group guidance	Weekly
Leisure projects		Weekly
Consultation with nurse	Individual counseling	Weekly
County options program	Individual counseling	Biweekly
Department of social services	Individual counseling	Biweekly
Women, Infants, and Children Clinic	Nutrition education	Monthly
Group meals		Occasionally
Adoption panel		Semester
Student workshop day		Semester

bring their children with them to the cooperative alternative education program. This posed several problems:

- How were the infants to be transported to the cooperative program's campus?
- Once the infants arrived, who would care for them and where would they be cared for?
- How would having infants in school affect the mother's schoolwork?

The issue of transportation proved complicated but was eventually solved. The young mothers would be allowed to ride the special-education school buses with their children. It was determined for insurance purposes and based on school policy that anyone associated with the instructional program for students could be allowed access to the school buses. The young mothers would be learning child care skills by caring for their infants, and the infants would be "students" in the sense that they were engaging in learning from their mothers and other child care staff. The children would be required to ride in car seats strapped into the bus seat. Since the teen mothers would be using special-education buses, the seats were equipped with seat belts and other devices, to provide for their special needs.

However, this transportation arrangement sometimes required additional costs. While pregnant, the teen mother-to-be rode on the regular school bus; however, once her child was born and the student was ready to return to school, a special-education bus would have to be rerouted or newly assigned to pick up the student and her child. This was no problem when the young mother lived on or near an existing special-education school bus route. If the young mother lived more than a set distance away from a normal route, other arrangements had to be made, and this created additional costs for the school district.

Once the issue of transportation was solved, the issue of location had to be resolved. The child care program was minimal at first and was housed in the same room where the student mothers did their schoolwork. Half the room was arranged into study carrels, and half the room was arranged as a nursery. A child care attendant was hired to care for the infants while the mothers and mothers-to-be did their schoolwork. The prevailing wisdom of the time was that the teen mothers and mothers-to-be would have an opportunity to observe appropriate care-giving skills modeled by the child care attendant. When assistance in care giving was required, mothers and mothers-to-be could be enlisted under the supervision of the child care attendant.

The location of the child care facility in the school building proved complicated because of licensing requirements. The department of social services had no jurisdiction over school buildings, so it could not license school districts; on the other hand, a license was required for the facility to receive child care funds from the department. This dilemma proved to be a catch-22. Careful negotiations and a change in legislative guidelines were required for the creation of a child care facility within the school building. In the meantime, the child care facility, located in one half of a classroom, followed the department of social services' guidelines when possible. For example, the ratio of infants to staff, the distance between cribs, and the amount of floor space for play per infant were maintained. Other child care requirements and arrangements are presented in appendix K.

This arrangement proved quite useful in a number of ways. The teen mothers reported that they learned a lot from observing the child care attendant in action. The child care attendant stated that she was able to assist the young mothers when they had questions about appropriate child care techniques. Even when the infants cried, lessons could be learned by both the mother and mother-to-be on how to handle the stress of a crying child.

An unexpected problem arose when a very young mother (twelve years old and in seventh grade) insisted on holding her child continuously in the classroom. She stated that if the child were at home, her mother would be holding the baby while she did the household chores throughout the day. It was the custom of her family that infants were either in the arms of a family member or in the crib. If her child was not being held by the child care attendant, the mother wanted to hold the child. This proved too distracting for the teachers and created dissension among the other students. She eventually dropped out of the program. In an effort to provide child care services to the young mothers, scarce space was utilized to the breaking point: teen mothers attempted to do their schoolwork while their children were cared for by a child care attendant, and teachers tried to work with students while infants cried in another part of the room. Had we created an impossible situation or a microcosm of the real world? Had necessity forced us to create a theory of child care role modeling? Was practice somehow influencing the way we thought about child care or were we merely justifying our simplistic efforts to find child care solutions to a very complex problem? It was difficult to assess how our efforts to assist mothers in completing their education in this half classroom, half day care center influenced the development of both mother and child.

This was not an isolated case. As other programs for pregnant and parenting students get underway (very often with limited space, staff, and resources), the staff are called upon to make similar decisions on a regular basis. When there is limited access to existing research and when new questions emerging from practice are not even addressed by the research, where do well-meaning practitioners go for help in determining the consequences of the trade-offs they have made in trying to help clients? How can theory inform practice and how can practice articulate the questions that are being addressed on a daily basis in the schools and programs designed for pregnant and parenting teens?

As a result of an increase in the program's enrollment, a separate room was designated as a child care facility and additional child care attendants were hired.

Counseling

As part of a cooperative educational setting, counselors were available for the teen parents at the cooperative school and at the student's regular school. Additional mental health services were available by referral to the community mental health system.

Health Care

In response to the medical needs of the pregnant and parenting teens attending the cooperative program, a referral system was designed in which the school nurse was the point of contact. The health component was composed of three segments: the school nurse's activities; a Women, Infants, and Children (WIC) clinic; and outside speakers invited to conduct workshops and classes on topics identified as important by the students or staff.

As the focal point of the health component, the nurse not only provided formal classes on various aspects of pregnancy but also conducted routine examinations of the children in the child care center. The school nurse also determined the severity of the adolescents' health-related complaints and made the decision whether a student was to be sent home early from school or needed to rest on the cots provided in the school building, whether a doctor was to be called, or whether an ambulance was necessary.

The WIC clinic was located on the campus. In this way students would not have to miss a whole day of school in order to attend a WIC clinic. (For additional information regarding WIC programs, see chapter 8.) These clinics provide blood testing, vouchers for specific food products, nutrition counseling, and periodic physical examinations of the infants and children. However, as financial resources became scarce, the clinic was discontinued on the school site. The teen mothers had to leave school for this service, and this added to their already high rate of absenteeism.

The health care component was enhanced by periodic speakers, who made presentations and conducted series of special topics for the students. These topics included child care, breast-feeding, smoking, substance abuse, and contraception. Most of these special sessions were conducted by staff members from outside agencies, were arranged verbally, and were confirmed through a letter of agreement.

The mental health needs of students attending the cooperative alternative education program were handled through referrals to the school counselors and outside agencies. However, many of the daily emotional issues were handled by the teachers and staff of the program. Because the faculty-to-student ratio was smaller than in a traditional classroom setting, students and faculty had an opportunity to interact on a regular and personal basis, often eating lunch together and working one-on-one on projects such as journal writing. Because of this close involvement, teachers and students learned to interact with each other. As in any relationship, there was a give-and-take on both sides; some relationships proved beneficial and helpful; other relationships ended in the student returning to the home school or dropping out. It was through this daily interaction that greater mental health problems were identified and referrals to the school counselor and outside organizations were made.

Referrals to child protective services were included in this referral system. However, a referral was generally made in the presence of the teen mother and with her permission. In most cases, the referrals were made because the pregnant and parenting teen was being abused by the significant male in her life. In cases in which we identified evidence of potential child abuse through marks on the child's body, appropriate referrals were made through the school nurse.

Vocational Training

Students attending the alternative education program in the cooperative setting did so at the vocational campus. Therefore, they had the opportunity to attend vocational classes. Several teen parents were enrolled in business, cosmetology, retailing, horticulture, and auto mechanics classes, among others.

Part IV

Conclusion

Chapter Fourteen
Recent Trends

As the end of the twentieth century approaches, changes in society appear to be flowing swiftly and in different directions. Educational programs for pregnant and parenting teens seem to be at the center of some changes and caught in the wake of others. Birth is the central act of our humanity. Giving life and caring for our children and our families is at the core of our daily life. Pregnant and parenting teenagers are therefore today's lightening rod and seem to attract the emotional, psychological, and metaphysical concerns of the general population.

C.J. Jung spent his lifework describing the myths and images that affect the processes by which we come to self-acceptance. One of the most powerful images is that of mother and child. It is a truism to say that we are all someone's child. Therefore the maternal image has been portrayed in art for centuries; we are moved by pictures of mothers with their children in all kinds of settings: running together in a field, a mother watching her child attached to tubes and mechanical devices in a hospital, mothers nursing their children. We all have our own image of motherhood, and we each understand in our own way the meaning of the word "mother."

A teenager with a baby somehow creates in us a dissonance with many of our images of motherhood. As a result of this dissonance, our collective response to pregnant and parenting teenagers has been schizophrenic. On the one hand, we want to be supportive of motherhood; on the other, we want to punish teenage mothers, who seem to defile the image we have of motherhood. The programs we offer pregnant and parenting teens span the continuum between these two extremes. We often give with one hand but take away with the other. For example, we provide special educational programs for pregnant and parenting teens while they are in high school, but just when they seem to be getting ahead, we no longer have any means of supporting them because they have graduated from school—after all, it is only a high school program. Or we write regulations regarding attendance at special programs for pregnant and parenting teens, and these regulations require a fifteen-year-old young woman to return to school two weeks after the birth of her child and do not provide any guidance on how or where to secure day care. Within this schizophrenic approach to service delivery, pregnant and parenting teens and their children and families live out their daily lives, and these lives will be affected by the concrete changes that are taking place within society and within the educational reform movement.

Within society, at least four major trends are now influencing programs for pregnant and parenting teens and their families: welfare reform, changes in the health care system, the desire for less federal government intervention in the lives of citizens, and the phenomenon of multiculturalism.

As this book is being written, welfare reform is being debated in the United States Congress and state governments are legislating changes to state-supported financial assistance programs. The outcome of these reforms and their impact on individual lives has yet to be determined. However, the reforms seem to be sending mixed signals on the importance of familial relationships. On the one hand, women are being encouraged to stay home and raise their children, yet on the other, some welfare reform programs stress the importance of working for the financial assistance provided through welfare.[1] The teen mother is caught in a catch-22. If she wants to stay home and raise her child, she may be called a freeloader—only on welfare for the money. If she decides to go to work, she may be forced to leave her children in unsafe conditions because of lack of day care options, in which case she is considered a neglectful mother, one who is "selfishly only thinking of her career," as some critics may add.

The recent welfare reforms also reflect society's current attitudes toward the role of the father in raising children. There is a lot of current rhetoric about the importance of fathers, but it does not seem to translate itself into action. Mothers are being asked to sign statements regarding the rearing of their children in order to receive welfare. Similar statements are not being asked of fathers. Complex familial relationships play a significant role in welfare reform. Yet these familial relationships are deeply personal and value-laden. The term *family* means different things to different people. Although this may be obvious to some, creating a welfare reform policy that acknowledges familial differences may prove challenging if not impossible. There is a deep concern among many individuals who work with pregnant and parenting teens that welfare reform, instead of acknowledging diverse family structures, will mandate policies that benefit only those who fit a rigid definition of family.

Pregnant and parenting teens are also influenced by recent reforms in the health care system. Yet, although women's issues in health care are beginning to be considered important in the areas of research and practice, they are a long way from being fully addressed. As the health care system moves more and more into a private, for-profit mode, individuals without health insurance (i.e., the working poor with limited coverage and other individuals unable to pay for adequate health care) may be in jeopardy of losing their lives because of poor health care. Teen mothers and their families are caught up in the health care reform movement, but at the same time, some children of teen parents are in intensive-care, neonatal units because of the poor nutrition, drug and alcohol abuse, and other health problems of the mother during her pregnancy. And even if health care is provided for pregnant and parenting teens and their children, little attention is being paid to the non-pregnancy-related health care needs of young mothers, as the research described in chapter 5 showed. Changes in health care will have a profound effect on teen parents and their families.

The public debate over the role of government in the lives of its citizens is another significant issue for pregnant and parenting teens. Determining whether federal dollars are to be regulated and administered through federal agencies or through block grants to states is an interesting policy debate that has a direct impact on the programs and services for these teenagers and their families.

Finally, the recent debate over the issues of immigration, assimilation, and acceptance of diversity while "one nation under God" is maintained has a profound effect on pregnant and parenting teens and their families. The debate concerns who is an American. Providing services for immigrants' children born in the United States creates a dilemma for politicians and citizens alike who want to care for the needs of young children yet safeguard jobs for American citizens. This debate is at the very foundation of our country's heritage. Pregnant and parenting teens and their children, both citizens and immigrants, are caught up in this debate and their lives are affected by the policies that result from the differing points of view on this issue.

Not only social trends but also educational reforms affect the pregnant and parenting student and her family. Innovations such as year-round schools, full-service schools, distance education, single-sex schools, and school-community partnerships can both challenge and enhance educational programs for these teenagers.

Year-round schools can prove to be a positive experience for pregnant and parenting teens who have in the past been required to repeat a whole school year because of excessive absences. If the year-round school also includes a revolving curriculum in which units of study are taught in shorter segments, so that excessive absences in one learning cycle do not negate success in other learning cycles, year-round schools could enable pregnant and parenting teens to repeat a learning cycle and not be penalized for time spent on maternity leave.

Full-service schools, if adopted, could benefit pregnant and parenting teens. Dryfoos (1994) describes full-service schools as a movement to create an array of integrated support services for schools that respond to the declining welfare of many American families and the rising "new morbidities" of sex, drugs, violence, and stress among youth. Through this approach, a new environment is created in the schools and brings together all the services that children, youth, and families need to live productive lives. This type of school reform places adolescent pregnancy and parenting within a holistic context. Adolescent parenting is only one of many life situations that require special attention. Just as youth who are physically challenged require special services (e.g., health care and physical adaptations), teenagers who are pregnant or parenting require services unique to their life situation. Pregnant and parenting teens should do well in full-service schools.

Distance education can also be a boon for pregnant and parenting teens. As computers, electronic media, and other technological advances become more available, pregnant and parenting teens could benefit from them. It would be possible for a pregnant teen who is bedridden to continue her class work through electronic mail, video programs, and other technological devices.

Another issue, single-sex schools, does not apply here, since alternative education programs for pregnant and parenting teens have generally centered around teen mothers. However, the debate about the benefits of single-sex schools goes beyond programs for pregnant and parenting teens. Some of the young women I interviewed in my research study and other pregnant and parenting teens I have talked to in the past several years believe that they receive a better education in schools where they do not have to worry about interacting with young men on a daily basis and can concentrate on their schoolwork. In a recent study, the American Association of University Women presented evidence that young women who attend single-sex schools can excel academically. As the debate over single-sex schools continues, alternative education programs for pregnant and parenting young women will also continue. A question arises about the creation of alternative education programs for young men who are teen fathers. If teen fathers can be identified, would it be appropriate for them to attend a special alternative school designed to help them complete high school and learn parenting skills in the same way that young women are asked to attend alternative schools geared toward their needs? With the increased societal emphasis on the importance of fathers in the development of their children, would such alternative programs for teen fathers be appropriate? It is not within the scope of this book to resolve this debate but to situate the alternative education programs for pregnant and parenting teens within the context of educational reform.

The final recent topic in educational reform concerns the importance of school-community relationships. This is particularly important to pregnant and parenting teens. The needs of pregnant and parenting teens are often so great that a number of organizations and agencies within a community have contact with adolescent parents, and they include the department of social services, hospitals, counseling services, grocery stores, stores that sell baby items and adolescent-connected items (clothing, audio-video materials, and books), recreational centers, youth-serving organizations, and churches. One of the driving forces within the adolescent pregnancy prevention and services movement has been the securing of comprehensive services for pregnant and parenting teens. Therefore any educational reform that encourages greater involvement from the community (including human service agencies, business organizations, and other community groups) would certainly be valuable.

Alternative education programs for pregnant and parenting teens and their families are affected by the social issues and educational reforms of the 1990s. Although many of these programs for pregnant and parenting teens have been around for over twenty years (as is the case with the alternative education program discussed in chapters 3 through 9), an atmosphere of transition exists within society during these later years of the twentieth century.

At least since the 1960s, service providers have been concerned with the needs of pregnant and parenting teens. The fact that unwed pregnancy and parenting has become the focal point of welfare reform, health care reform, and other social changes could prove to be a disaster, but if the voices of the various stakeholders within the system can be heard and heeded, then perhaps these waves of social change will result in better and more comprehensive services for pregnant and parenting teens and their families.

Note

1.   See Aber, Brooks-Gunn, and Maynard (1995) for a discussion of welfare reform and teenage pregnancy.

Chapter Fifteen
Points to Consider

In this book, an effort has been made to describe a dynamic system of service delivery. The service-delivery systems associated with the education of pregnant and parenting teens are vital because the range of their services change over time. These systems are also dynamic because of the interplay of the various stakeholders who move through and around the systems and because the systems deal with the lives of young women and their families. These three dialectics of the changing range of services, the involvement of various stakeholders, and the life histories of teen mothers and their families create the dynamism of educational service-delivery systems to pregnant and parenting teens.

Range of Services over Time

The importance of consistency over time in the range of services offered in a particular program emerged not just from my research but was also echoed from practice. Although programs evolve over time, and that contributes to their dynamism, the type of services required by pregnant and parenting teens (i.e., academics, child care, transportation, employment opportunities, etc.) generally remains constant. The service providers I interviewed reported that they offered these services to their clients either through referrals, directly, or spontaneously when the services were lacking within a given system. Once in place, these methods form a safety net that the provider uses to guide a young mother in securing services.

One of the most significant findings from my research was that services to pregnant and parenting teens are limited to those enrolled in specific programs through the school and are usually available only until graduation. A large segment of teen mothers do not receive services because they have dropped out or graduated from school. It is precisely at this point that teen mothers may be having their second child or, as their child gets older, they may need support and services. Therefore, the basic services available to young parents of high school age need to be extended to young parents making the transition from high school to the world of adulthood and work, college, or marriage.

Stakeholders

From my interviews with the various stakeholders presented in chapters 5 through 9, several recommendations for service-delivery systems emerged.

First, the need for one consistent caseworker and direct-service provider over time was reported by teen parents, their support people, and the direct-service providers. It is extremely helpful to have a consistent contact person for the young mother at the point of interface between the client and the system. This consistency is particularly important for young mothers under the age of fifteen who require developmentally appropriate services that focus on young adolescent needs.

For this to occur, several things need to happen:

- Direct-service providers (including teachers, social workers, medical personnel, and any other professionals who have direct contact with the teen mother) need to be familiar with other services within the community, trained in youth development, and trained in collaborative techniques in order to work with service providers from other organizations.
- In order to retain professional levels of service, funding needs to be in place to compensate direct providers at above the minimum wage.
- The work of direct-service providers needs to be valued as the essential contact point in a service-delivery system—the place where the client meets and interacts with the system.

Second, creative ways of supporting the "significant others" in teen parents' lives need to be encouraged. Self-help groups for the parents of teen parents, counseling for the support people, and parenting classes for males were among the suggestions proposed by the family support members interviewed. Third, the basic services need to be extended to young parents nineteen to twenty-three years of age.

The importance of the direct-service provider cannot be overstated. The direct-service provider is the point of contact for the whole service-delivery system. A caring service provider was viewed by the pregnant and parenting teens interviewed as one of the most significant factors in their receiving maximum benefit from the services provided by the community. This confirms much of the research on adolescents, which advocates the need for at least one caring adult in the life of a young person (Scales1991).

These three recommendations fly in the face of today's political climate, which demands major cuts in programs for young mothers and their children. However, from a business sense the one way to make money is to invest existing dollars. Therefore, the only way to create a successful citizenry is to invest in that citizenry as early as possible. That means when the citizens are children. The children of teen parents are part of the voting citizenry of the future and part of the fabric of the country today.

Lives of Teen Parents and Their Families

The most significant thing I learned both from my research and from the years of working with pregnant and parenting teens and their families, again, is that *adolescent parenting is not a problem to be solved but a reality to be lived.* Children are part of our lives. They are not problems.

The lives of pregnant and parenting teens are filled with real suffering and, often, insurmountable problems. In particular, recent research has made it extremely evident that many of our young women have become parents as a result of victimization by older men (Boyer 1995). This cannot be overlooked. It is an underlying premise of my work that creating caring environments for young people requires the strength and commitment of dedicated adults to help adolescents face the challenges in their everyday lives.

It is hoped that through this book, those who work with pregnant and parenting teens and their families may find the strength and encouragement to continue, and to inspire others to continue, in this rewarding, if difficult task.

Appendices

Appendix A
Research Design

Questions	Data Collection	Analysis
Phase 1: National Context		
1. What is the stated formal policy?	Interview policy elite	1. Read transcripts, observation notes, and documents
2. What is the informal policy?	Observe (appendix B):	2. Develop codes/categories based on questions
3. What are the barriers to service?	1. Policy elite interacting with staff	3. Code/categorize data
4. How can service be enhanced?	2. Interactions in lobby, waiting room	4. Review data
	3. Policy elite interaction at conferences	
	4. Policy elite at board meeting	
	Document review (appendix C):	
	1. Interagency material	
	2. National policy material	
Phase 2: Local Level		
Stage 1—Community Demographics and Key Variables		
1. What services exist?	A. Review documents (appendix C):	Content analysis
2. Location of service	1. Site materials	
3. Geographical distribution of clients vs. services	2. Individualized client materials	
4. Characteristics of clients	3. Service providers' materials	
	4. Program administration	
	5. Interagency material	
	B. Community demographics material (appendix D)	

Stage 2—Input from Clients and Members of Their Support System

1. What are the needs of the client?
2. How are those needs being met?
3. Who helps the client?
4. What are the needs of the support person?
5. What barriers exist to the service deliverer?
6. What strategies facilitate service delivery?

1. Focused group interviews of self-selected
   (a) clients, (b) clients and support persons, and
   (c) support persons
2. Individual interviews
3. Survey developed with input of clients for distribution to clients not participating in focused interview
4. Observe:
   (a) Interaction between clients and their family and friends at clients' home
   (b) Interaction of public and service providers at service-delivery sites

1. Read transcripts, observation notes, and documents
2. Develop codes/categories based on questions
3. Reread data
4. Adjust codes
5. Code/categorize data

Stage 3—Input from Program Administrators and Service Providers

1. Do gaps in service exist?
2. Which models of service delivery lessen these gaps?
3. How do individuals within the service-delivery system cope with policy changes?
4. What linkages between individuals and organizations create a comprehensive service-delivery system?

Interviews with program administrators and service providers

1. Content analysis of interview transcriptions
2. Comparison of data to various theoretical models

Appendix B
Protocol for Interviews with Policymakers

1. How did you get interested in the adolescent parenting issues?
2. What role do you see yourself playing in the service-delivery system to parenting adolescents?
3. Describe a parenting adolescent success story that you were a part of.
4. What are some things that make your work difficult?
5. What programs and policies related to adolescent parenting do you particularly oversee?
6. How are you evaluating programs and policies?
7. What problems have you identified?
8. How are you planning to overcome these problems?
9. How do you deal with conflicting policies from other governmental agencies?
10. What types of mechanisms are in place for sharing information with other agencies?
11. If you had all the money you needed, how would you change the present policies and programs for parenting adolescents?

Appendix C
Community Demographic Data Sheet
Documents and Archival Materials Checklist

Community Demographic Data Sheet

Location: _____ Dates of visit: _____

1. Sources of information:
2. Population of community:
3. Area in square miles:
4. Average family income:
5. Percentage below poverty level:
6. Economic life-style:
7. What is the distance of the community from—
   a. State capital?
   b. County seat?
8. What types of organizations are available in the community for—
   a. Recreation?
   b. Shopping?
   c. Laundry?
   d. Housing?
   e. Newspaper?
   f. Broadcasting?

Documents and Archival Materials Checklist

Site:
- Map
- Community newspaper
- Church announcements
- Bus/transportation schedules
- Other

Individual:

- Consent form

Service providers:

- Job descriptions
- Forms used with clients
- Forms used within the agency
- Policy and/or procedure manuals
- Referral forms
- Handbooks
- Work schedules
- Other

Program administrators:

- Annual report
- Program brochures
- Publicity materials
- Other

Interagency materials:

- Referral forms
- Membership material
- Minutes of meetings
- By-laws
- Rules of procedure
- Other

National policy materials:

- Legislative memoranda
- Public laws
- Guidelines for request for proposals
- Minutes of legislative committee hearings
- Other

Appendix D
Data Sheets for Clients and Family Support

Client and Family Support System Data Sheet

Code name _____ Location _____ Date _____

Street address _____ Date of birth _____

Number of individuals in household and relationship to teen parent:

1.

2.

3.

4.

5.

Marital status and relationship with baby's father

Employment

Education

Physical condition

Financial situation

Other

Legal guardian _____ Relationship _____

Child's birth date _____ At birth Ht. _____ Wt. _____

Present Ht. _____ Wt. _____

Feeding information

Child care arrangements

Physical condition

Other

Client and Family Support System Interview Data Sheet

Location _____ Date _____

Service	Needed	Received	Where	Who Helps	Comments
Food					
Clothing					
Shelter					
Physical Health					
Mental Health					
Education					
Vocational Training					
Socializing / Recreation					
Finances					
Transpor- tation					
Child Care					
Employ- ment					
Religious Affiliation					
Other					

Appendix E
Survey of Students

April 6, 1990

Dear Teen Parent:

We are requesting your participation in a confidential survey to help us understand your needs as a teen parent. We need your help to enable us to identify the services teen parents need and receive. Please fill out the enclosed questionnaire and return it to us in the enclosed stamped envelope as soon as possible.

Thank you for your time and participation. It is greatly appreciated.

Sincerely,
The Senior Class

Enclosure

Survey of Teen Parents

Do Not Leave Your Name

How old are you? _____

Are you still pregnant?   yes / no

What are the ages of your child(ren)? _____

1. Which of these services do you receive for food?

   WIC .... yes / no

   Food stamps ... yes / no

   Parents .... yes / no

   Boyfriend .... yes / no

   Other _____

   Comment: _____

   _____

2. Do you need clothing for yourself?   yes / no

   your child(ren)?   yes / no

   If yes, do you know where to look for help?   yes / no

   Comment: _____

   _____

3. Do you have appropriate (adequate) shelter?   yes / no

   If yes, who or what services provide shelter for you?

   Comment: _____

   _____

4. Do you receive adequate health care? yes / no

   If no, what services do you need?

   Comment: _____

   _____

5. Do you have someone to talk to in a stressful situation?

   yes / no

   If a friend or member of your family needed mental help,

   would you know where to go for help?   yes / no

   Comment: _____

   _____

6. Are you presently attending school?   yes / no

   If yes, circle the grade you're presently in:

   7   8   9   10   11   12   college

   If no, circle the last year completed:

   7   8   9   10   11   12   college

If you would like to return to school, do you know where to go for information?   yes / no

7. Have you ever attended vocational courses?   yes / no

If interested, do you know where to go for more information? yes / no

Comment: _____

_____

8. How much time do you have to yourself a day? (Check the ones that apply.)

No time _____

1–2 hours _____

3–5 hours _____

Other _____

Comment: _____

_____

How do you spend your free time? _____

_____

I'm limited in my free-time activities due to (Check the ones that apply):

1. No transportation _____

2. Lack of money _____

3. No baby-sitter _____

4. Other _____

Comment: _____

_____

9. Which of the following do you receive? (Check the ones that apply.)

Welfare _____   Job   _____

Medicaid _____   Alimony   _____

WIC _____   Child support _____

Other _____

Do you need additional financial assistance?   yes / no

Comment: _____

_____

10. Do you own a car?   yes / no
If no, how do you get from one place to another? (Check the
ones that apply.)
Boyfriend   _____
Bus   _____
Taxi   _____
Family   _____
Friends   _____
Other   _____
Which do you use the most? _____
Comment: _____
_____

11. What type of child care do you have? (Check the ones that
apply.)
Day care   _____
Friend   _____
Family   _____
Boyfriend   _____
Other   _____
None   _____
If none, do you need day care?   yes / no
Comment: _____
_____

12. Are you employed?   yes / no
If no, are you looking for a job?   yes / no
Comment: _____
_____

13. Do you belong to a religious organization?   yes / no
If yes, which one? _____
During your pregnancy how were you treated by your church?
Comment: _____
_____

14. Do you still have a relationship with your child's father?
yes / no
If yes, is it (check one)   ___ very poor? ___ poor? ___fair?
___ good? ___ very good?
Does he display an active role in raising his child?   yes / no

11. What are the difficulties involved in working with other agencies that have the same client?
12. Describe a successful client intervention.
13. What are the barriers you face in serving your clients?
14. What could your agency do to overcome these barriers?
15. What could other agencies, the community, and the parenting adolescents do to overcome these barriers?
16. What types of professional organizations do you belong to that help you deal with parenting adolescents?
17. Other comments about the service-delivery system.

Appendix G
Protocol for Interviews with Program Administrators

1. Organization
2. Years in this position
3. Background and history of employment
4. What prompted you to enter the field of human service?
5. How does your organization fit into the overall pattern of services to pregnant adolescents in this community?
6. How are services to adolescents under the age of fifteen different from those given to the "normal clients"?
7. How do you handle clients who require services that you don't provide?
8. Describe a "successful case."
9. Describe the barriers to service in your community.
10. What type of services do the service providers receive, to help them in their jobs and personal lives?
11. What professional and/or community organizations are you involved in? In which do you hold leadership roles?
12. What types of public relations activities does your agency conduct?

Appendix H
Form for Observational Notes

Date _____

Time	Individuals	Environment	Interaction	Comments

Appendix I

Tutorial Procedures and Forms

I. Application for Enrollment
   A) Filled out by student and includes:
      1) Doctor's statement confirming pregnancy
      2) Parent or guardian's signature
      3) School district official's signature
   B) Once this form is received, the Teenage Pregnancy Program instructor makes an appointment to meet with the student's home school teachers.

II. Subject Information (Triplicate)
   A) Filled out by each home school teacher at the above-mentioned meeting (one form for each subject for each student).
   B) Signed by home school teacher and Teenage Pregnancy Program instructor.
   C) *Copy 1*—Placed in student subject folder.
      Copy 2—Home school instructor.
      Copy 3—Teenage Pregnancy Program instructor.

III. Student Schedule
   A) Filled out daily by each student based on her individual assignments and activities.
   B) Group activities, lunch, and other common projects are scheduled at the beginning of the week.
   C) Handed in at the end of each week.

IV. Daily Food Diary
   A) Filled out by each student daily.
   B) Handed in at the end of week.

V. Assignment Sheets (Triplicate)
   A) Filled in by Teenage Pregnancy Program instructor when returning or requesting assignments.

    B) *Copy 1*—Kept by Teenage Pregnancy Program instructor and placed in student's subject folder.

       Copy 2 and *Copy 3*—Sent to home school teacher.

       Copy 3—Returned to Teenage Pregnancy Program instructor with new assignment.

VI. Special Report (Triplicate)

    A) Filled out by Teenage Pregnancy Program instructor at the end of each marking period.

    B) One for each subject for each student.

    C) *Copy 1*—Sent to home school teacher.

       Copy 2—Given to student.

       Copy 3—Kept in student's subject folder.

VII. Not included here are:

    A) Permanent record cards.

    B) Follow-up questionnaires.

    C) Other research-related materials.

Official Application for Enrollment

Please provide the following information and return it to the above address. A student cannot begin attendance in the Program for Pregnant Teens until the information has been returned.

Student Name _____   School District _____

Address   _____   Address _____

Telephone   _____   Contact Person _____

Age of Student _____   Telephone _____

Date of Birth   _____

Date Attendance Is to Begin _____

Expected Delivery Date _____

Doctor's Name and Address   _____

_____

_____

Telephone   _____

Please attach a copy of doctor's statement confirming pregnancy!

Student Grade Level

Subject	*Teacher*
1. _____	_____
2. _____	_____
3. _____	_____
4. _____	_____
5. _____	_____

Signature of School District Official _____

Signature of Parent or Guardian _____

Please fill in the following information, checking the appropriate ways you would like your student tutored.

Subject Information

Student _____ Subject _____

Grade _____ Teacher _____

Academic Ability (check one): Telephone _____

A B C D F Unknown

Teacher available for consultation: Free period _____ to _____

After school _____

Home _____

Title of Textbook _____

Subject Information

Other Curricular Materials   _____

_____

_____

_____

Assignments will be sent (check one):	Check the materials to be used:
1) Weekly	Course outline _____
2) Biweekly	Textbook _____
3) Chapters, in units	Teacher's edition _____
4) For the whole semester (include outline)	Answer key _____
5) Other _____	Workbooks _____
	Other _____
	Films _____

Return assignments (check one):
1) Weekly
2) Biweekly
3) Chapters, in units
4) Quarterly
5) At end of semester (only)
6) Other _____

Grading (check one):   Comments: Please feel free to make
  Teacher will grade all assignments __   other arrangements not
  Tutor will grade all assignments __   included in the above list.
  Tutor will grade under the direction
  of teacher   _____

  _____   _____

          (Be specific)   _____

  Other _____   _____

  _____   _____

        Teacher Signature   Date

Student Schedule

Name _____ Week of _____

Time	Monday	Tuesday	Wed.	Thursday	Friday
A.M. 9:00–9:30					
9:30–10:00					
10:00–10:30					
10:30–11:00					
11:00–11:30					
11:30–12:00					
P.M. 12:30–1:00					
1:00–1:30					
1:30–2:00					
Home Time					

Daily Food Diary

Week of _____ Name _____

	Monday	Tuesday	Wed.	Thursday	Friday
Breakfast					
Snack					
Lunch					
Snack					
Supper					
Snack					
Meat 2–3					
Milk 2–3					
Fruits 2–4 and Veg. 3–5					
Bread 6–11					

Special Report

_____ Date

_____ Days Absent

Student _____

       (last name)   (first name)

Grade Level _____

Present Class Average _____

Home School _____

Teacher _____

This is a report to notify you of _____'s progress in _____.
The comments checked below specifically indicate areas of strength
and/or weakness.

Effort and Behavior:
( ) Shows consistent effort
( ) Seeks help when
    needed
( ) Is conscientious in
    completing work
( ) Needs to be more
    attentive and to follow
    directions more carefully
( ) Needs improvement in
    effort or consistency of
    effort
( ) Needs to seek help when
    needed

Classroom Achievement:
( ) Is consistently prepared
    for and on time to class
( ) Follows directions well
    and is cooperative
( ) Works well independently
( ) Written work is late or
    incomplete
( ) Inadequate preparation
    for tests
( ) Frequent absences hamper
    progress and continuity

Quality of Work:
( ) Work is consistently
    of high quality (beyond
    course requirements)
( ) Work is consistently
    of good quality (meets
    course requirements)
( ) Work is in need of
    improvement (below
    course requirements)

Comments: _____

_____

_____

If you feel the need to discuss this report in person, please call.

_____

                 (Instructor)

Teacher/Tutor/Student Assignment Sheet

To _____   Date _____

Re _____   Subject _____

The following material is being returned:

_____   Assignments   _____
_____   Work sheets   _____
_____   Test   _____
_____   Textbook   _____
_____   Answer key   _____
_____   Map   _____
_____   Equipment   _____
_____   Other   _____

Comments: _____

_____

_____

Please forward to:

_____   Assignments   _____
_____   Work sheets   _____
_____   Test   _____
_____   Textbook   _____
_____   Answer key   _____
_____   Map   _____
_____   Equipment   _____
_____   Other   _____

Comments: _____

_____

_____

Check below:

_____   Return original copy
_____   Duplicate copy (your files)

Appendix J
Demographics for Client Living Arrangements
and the Outreach Program

Groups Defined

Group   I: Residing with single parent.

Group   II: Residing with both parents.

Group   III: Residing with other relative, with friend, or under restrictive care.

Group   IV: Single teen mother—own household.

Group   V: Married teen mother—residing with spouse.

Client Living Arrangements

Group   I: *27%* of the adolescent mothers could only rely on a single mother (many of whom were mothers under stress), while *1.3%* resided with a single father.

Group   II: *30.6%* of the adolescent mothers resided with both their mother and father.

Group   III: *4.3%* of the adolescent mothers lived with a relative and *0.4%* with a friend, while *1.7%* lived in residential care.

Group   IV: *17.4%* of the single adolescent mothers set up their own households and relied solely on public assistance.

Group   V: *4.3%* of the adolescent mothers were married, while *13%* were living with the father of their child (or a young man who assumed that role).

Outreach Program

Group   I: *18.5%* of the adolescent mothers could only rely on a single mother, while *3.8%* resided with a single father.

Group   II: *15.6%* of the adolescent mothers resided with both their mother and father.

Group III: *3.2%* of the adolescent mothers lived with a relative, while *1.0%* lived with a foster care family.

Group IV: *21.7%* of the single adolescent mothers had set up their own households.

Group V: *14.2%* of the adolescent mothers were married, while *22%* were living with the father of their child (or a young man who assumed that role).

Appendix K
Child Care Requirements

Nursery Guidelines

A. Food
1. Fill bottles to desired feeding amount; leave in refrigerator.
2. Put your child's first name on all bottles, food jars, etc.
3. Provide all food for your child.
4. Toddlers' parents are to provide snacks periodically for the 10:15 nursery snack (crackers, fresh fruit, dry cereal, cheese cubes, etc.). The feeding of infants and toddlers is to be completed before 9:00, between 11:30 and 1:00, or after 2:00.
5. Refrigerator provided for storage of children's food should be cleared daily. Leftover food must be stored in covered container.

B. Clothing
1. Leave 4 diapers and extra plastic pants on the shelf by your child's name each morning.
2. Bring 1 complete change of clothing for your child each day.
3. Hang outside clothes in your locker.
4. Leave a dry, clean child in the nursery at 9:00 and 12:45.

C. General
1. Keep your child's first name on your diaper bag.
2. Inform nursery staff of medication, feeding, and napping instructions.
3. Bring in toys for your child.
4. Medicines will be given only by the parent.

Items Needed for Child

Sheet for crib	(infant)
Receiving blanket	(infant)
Sweater	(infant or toddler)
Diapers—day's supply	(infant or toddler)
Plastic pants	(infant or toddler)
Formula or milk	(infant or toddler)
Cereal—solid food	(infant or toddler)
Special spoon and dish	(infant or toddler)
Change of clothing	(infant or toddler)
Special ointment	(infant or toddler)
Medicine	(infant or toddler)
Small blanket for naptime	(toddler)
Training pants, slacks, socks	(children being potty trained)

Label all articles with child's name.

If the mother brings special medication, it must be administered and kept by her.

Immunizations

Students with children attending the Teenage Pregnancy Program Infant Care Center will be required to have the medical forms filled out by the child's doctor and returned to the Center. A physical exam and up-to-date immunizations will be necessary for entrance into the day care program. Immunizations can be received from the child's doctor.

If the doctor has seen your child within the last eight weeks, it will not be necessary for you to have your child re-examined by him. However, the enclosed form must be taken into his office to be filled out and returned.

Medical Report of Day Care Child

State of . . .   Department of Social Services

NAME OF PERSON BEING EXAMINED   DATE OF BIRTH   DATE OF EXAMINATION

The above named child was examined and found to present no hazard from contagious and communicable disease, and is in good general health.

IMMUNIZATIONS

TYPE   DATE(S)   TYPE   DATE(S)

Tuberculin Test (Type)   Results

1. Are there allergic problems?   ___ Yes ___ No
   If yes, specify:

2. Is a special diet required?   ___ Yes ___ No
   If yes, specify:

3. Is medication regularly taken?   ___ Yes ___ No
   If yes, specify:

4. Are there any conditions requiring special attention by the day care provided?
   If yes, specify: ___ Yes ___ No

5. Condition of Teeth _____

6. Hearing Tested: Date _____ Method _____ Results: _____

7. Vision Tested: Date _____ Method _____ Results: _____

8. Mental growth and development ___ Normal ___ Abnormal
   If abnormal, describe:

9. Physical growth and development ___ Normal ___ Abnormal
   If abnormal, describe:

List any special recommendations about child's health
(use reverse side if necessary).

NAME OF PHYSICIAN (PLEASE PRINT)   SIGNATURE OF PHYSICIAN   ADDRESS
                                    X

Emergency Release Form*

I, _____, being the
parent or guardian of _____,
who will be attending the Teenage Pregnancy Program Infant Care
Center, do hereby consent to allow emergency medical treatment to
my child should such treatment become necessary during the periods of his/her attendance at the Center. I hereby give permission to
the nurse or staff of the Teenage Pregnancy Program Infant Care
Center the authority to consent, in my behalf, to any such medical
treatment. Dr. _____ is my regular doctor who cares for my
child.

_____
Parent

_____
Date

If living at home, grandparent or guardian must also sign the permission letter.

_____
Grandparent or Guardian

_____
Date

*Note: Return this signed form to the Teenage Pregnancy Program
Infant Care Center.

Appendix L

Alternative Education Center for Young Parents

Educational and Vocational Profile of 232 Cases (January through December 1989)

Educational Status of Pregnant Teens or Teen Mothers at the Start of 1989 Grant Year	Count	Pregnant Students/Student Mothers Enrolled at Alternative Jr. and Sr. High School Program during Grant Year	Remained at Alternative Jr. and Sr. High School Program	1989 Graduate	Enrolled at "Home" Jr. or Sr. High School	1989 Graduate at "Home School"	Enrolled in GED Program	Received 1989 GED Diploma	Remained in College	Remained in Business or Vocational Training Program	Home School or GED Graduate Remaining at Home	Not Enrolled in School (Dropouts)	Employed Full-Time	Youth Employment—Employed Part-Time	Employed in Training Program	Youth Employment	Not Employed	Not Employed (Attending School)
Educational/Employment Status of Clients at the End of the 1989 Grant Year																		
Junior High School Student	19	14	11	13	7	6	1	1	2	1	5	16	5	1	1	1		16
Senior High School Student	144	100	51		46		3							30		7	12	90
Enrolled in a Vocational Program	2	1								1		1		1				1
Enrolled in GED Program	3						2					1		2				1
Not Enrolled in School (Dropout)	51	5	5		1		13	6				26	4	5	3		18	21
High School or GED Graduate																		
Enrolled in College	3								3				1					2
Enrolled in a Vocational Program	3									3				1				2
Not Enrolled in Any Program	7												1	6				

References and Further Reading

References

Aber, J. Lawrence, Jeanne Brooks-Gunn, and Rebecca A. Maynard. (1995). Effects of welfare reform on teenage parents and their children. *Critical Issues for Children and Youths, 5.2,* 53–71.

Beck, Lynn. (1994). *Reclaiming educational administration as a caring profession* (foreword by Nel Noddings). Critical Issues in Educational Leadership Series, edited by Joseph Murphy. New York: Teachers College.

Bogenschneider, Karen, Stephen Small, and David Riley. (n.d.). *An ecological risk: focused approach for addressing youth-at-risk issues.* Developing Youth Potential. Chevy Chase, MD: National 4-H Center.

Boyer, Debra. (1995). The link between childhood victimization and teen pregnancy, part 1. *Child Welfare Report: Practical Solutions for Professionals, 3.8,* 5.

Center for Young Parents. (1990). 1989 statistical report. *The Buffalo News,* April 1, n.p.

Coles, Robert. (1989). *The call of stories: Teaching and the moral imagination.* Boston: Houghton Mifflin.

Compton, N., M. Duncan, and J. Hruska. (1987). *How schools can help combat student pregnancy.* Washington, DC: National Education Association Publication.

Deal, T., and A. Kennedy. (1982). *Corporate cultures: The rites and rituals of corporate life.* New York: Addison-Wesley.

Dryfoos, Joy G. (1994). *Full service schools: A revolution in health and social services for children, youth, and families.* San Francisco: Jossey-Bass.

Forrester, J. (1983). Critical theory and organizational analysis. In G. Morgan (ed.), *Beyond method: Strategies for social research,* 234–246. Beverly Hills, CA: Sage.

Hayes, C.D. (ed.). (1987). *Risking the future: Adolescent sexuality, pregnancy, and childbearing.* Washington, DC: National Academy Press, National Research Council.

Kelly, Deirdre M. (1993). *Last Chance High: How girls and boys drop in and out of alternative schools.* New Haven: Yale University Press.

Kelsey, M.J. (1981). *Caring: How can we love one another?* New York: Paulist.

Knapp, Michael S. (1995). How shall we study comprehensive, collaborative services for children and families? *Educational Researcher, 24.4,* 5–16.

Lerner, Richard M. (1995). *America's youth in crisis: Challenges and options for programs and policies.* Thousand Oaks, CA: Sage.

Lerner, Richard M., Karen Bogenschneider, Brian Wilcox, Ellen Fitzsimmons, and Leah Cox Hoopfer. (1995). *Welfare reform and the role of extension programming.* Institute for Children, Youth, and Families, Michigan State University. North Central Extension Directors.

Lindsay, Jeanne Warren. (1995). *School-age parents: The challenge of three-generation living.* Buena Park, CA: Morning Glory Press.

Lopez, B. (1987). *Arctic dreams: Imagination and desire in a northern landscape.* New York: Bantam.

Males, Mike. (1995). Adult men: The unspoken factor in teen pregnancy and disease. *PPT Express, 5.2,* 4.

Marecek, Mary. (1995). *Breaking free from partner abuse: Voices of battered women caught in the cycle of domestic violence.* Buena Park, CA: Morning Glory Press.

Marshall, C. (1985). Appropriate criteria of trustworthiness and goodness for qualitative research on education organizations. *Quality and Quantity, 19,* 353–373.

Mayeroff, M. (1971). On caring. Vol. 43 of *World perspectives,* edited by R.W. Anshen. New York: Harper.

Noddings, Nel. (1984). *Caring: A feminine approach to ethics and moral education.* Berkeley: University of California Press.

————. (1988). An ethic of caring and its implications for instructional arrangements. *American Journal of Education, 96.2,* 215–230.

————. (1989). Educating moral people. In M.M. Brabeck (ed.), *Who cares? Theory, research, and ethical implications of the ethic of care,* 216–233. New York: Praeger.

————. (1992). *The challenge to care in schools: Alternative approaches to education.* New York: Teachers College Press.

————. (1995). Teaching themes of care. *PHI Delta Kappan,* May, Volume 76, Number 9, 675–679.

Progoff, Ira. (1973). *The symbolic and the real: A new psychological approach to the fuller experience of personal existence.* New York: McGraw-Hill. (Originally published in 1963.)

Sarason, S.B. (1972). *The creation of settings and the future societies.* San Francisco: Jossey-Bass.

Scales, Peter C. (1991). *A portrait of young adolescents in the 1990s: Implications for promoting healthy growth and development.* Carrboro, NC: Center for Early Adolescence.

Vinovskis, M. (1988). *An epidemic of adolescent pregnancy? Some historical and policy considerations.* New York: Oxford University Press.

Weatherly, R., M. Levine, S. Perlman, and L. Kleiman. (1986). Comprehensive programs for pregnant teenagers and teenage parents. How successful can they be? *Family Planning Perspectives, 18.2,* 73–78.

————. (1987). National problems, local solutions: Comprehensive services for pregnant and parenting adolescents. *Youth and Services, 19.1.,* 73–92.

Wehlage, G.G. (1983). *Effective programs for the marginal high school student.* Bloomington, IN: Phi Delta Kappa.

Young, Timothy W. (1990). *Public alternative education: Options and choice for today's schools.* New York: Teachers College.

Further Reading

Adolescent Pregnancy

Allan, J., and D. Bender. (1980). *Managing teenage pregnancy: Access to abortion, contraception, and sex education.* New York: Praeger.

Atwood, Joan D., and William J. Donnelly. (1993). Adolescent pregnancy: Combating the problem from a multi-systemic health perspective. *Journal of Health Education, 24.4,* 219–227.

Belmont, L., P. Cohen, J. Dryfoos, Z. Stein, and S. Zayac. (1981). Maternal age and children's intelligence. In K. Scott, T. Field, and E. Robinson (eds.), *Teenage parents and their offspring,* 177–194. New York: Grune & Stratton.

Black, C., and R. De Blassie. (1985). Adolescent pregnancy: Contributing factors, consequences, treatment, plausible solutions. *Adolescence, 20.78,* 281–290.

Brindis, Claire D. (1991). *Adolescent pregnancy prevention: A guidebook for communities.* Palo Alto, CA: Health Promotion Resource Center.

Brindis, Claire D., and R. Jeremy. (1988). *Adolescent pregnancy and parenting in California: A strategic plan of action.* San Francisco: Center for Population and Reproductive Health Policy, University of California at San Francisco.

Card, Josefina. (1993). *Handbook of adolescent sexuality and pregnancy: Research and evaluation instruments.* Newbury Park, CA: Sage.

Center for Population Options. (1988). *Report estimates of public cost for teenage childbearing in 1987.* Washington, DC: Center for Population Options.

Chase-Lansdale, P. Lindsay, Jeanne Brooks-Gunn, and Roberta L. Paikoff. (1992). Research and programs for adolescent mothers: Missing links and future promises. *American Behavioral Scientist, 35.3,* 290–312.

Creighton-Zollar, Ann. (1990). *Adolescent pregnancy and parenthood: An annotated guide.* New York: Garland.

Dickman, I. (1981). *Teenage pregnancy: What can be done?* New York: Public Affairs Committee.

Furstenberg, F., R. Lincoln, and J. Menken. (1981). *Teenage sexuality, pregnancy and childbearing.* Philadelphia: University of Pennsylvania Press.

Furstenberg, G., J. Brooks-Gunn, and S.P. Morgan. (1987). *Adolescent mothers in later life.* New York: Cambridge University Press.

Governor's Task Force. (1986a). *Adolescent pregnancy: The challenge, a framework for prevention and parenting.* Augusta, ME: Maine Department of Human Services.

Governor's Task Force. (1986b). *Benchmarks and challenges: Third report of the governor's task force on adolescent pregnancy.* Albany, NY: Council on Children and Families.

Governor's Task Force on Adolescent Sexuality and Pregnancy. (1986). *Teenage pregnancy: Creating opportunity from crisis.* Ohio: State of Ohio.

Group for the Advancement of Psychiatry. (1986). *Crises of adolescence: Teenage pregnancy—impact on adolescent development* (Report No. 118). New York: Brunner/Mazel.

Gullotta, Thomas P., Gerald R. Adams, and Raymond Montemayor (eds.). (1993). *Adolescent sexuality*. Advances in Adolescent Development, 5. Newbury Park, CA: Sage.

Holt, K.A., and K. Langlykke (eds.). (1993). *Comprehensive adolescent pregnancy services: A resource guide*. Arlington, VA: National Center for Education in Maternal and Child Health.

Humenick, Sharron S., Norma N. Wilkerson, and Natalie W. Paul (1991). *Adolescent pregnancy: Nursing perspectives on prevention*. White Plains, NY: March of Dimes Birth Defect Foundation.

Jones, Dionne J., and Stanley F. Battle (eds.). (1990). *Teenage pregnancy: Developing strategies for change in the twenty-first century*. New Brunswick, NJ: Transaction.

Jones, E. (ed.). (1986). *Teenage pregnancy in industrial countries: A study sponsored by the Allan Guttmacher Institute*. New Haven, CT: Yale University Press.

Kinard, E.M., and H. Reinherz (1985). School aptitude achievement in children of adolescent mothers. *Journal of Youth and Adolescence, 16.1*, 69–87.

Klein, H., and A. Cordell (1987). The adolescent as mother: Early risk identification. *Journal of Youth and Adolescence, 16.1*, 47–58.

Klerman, L. (1981). Programs for pregnant adolescents and young parents: Their development and assessment. In K. Scott, T. Field, and E. Robertson (eds.), *Teenage parents and their offspring*, 227–248. New York: Grune and Stratton.

Klerman, L.V., and J.F. Jekel (1973). *School-age mothers: Problems, programs and policy*. Hamden, CT: Shoe String Press (Linnet).

Lacković-Grgin, Katica, and Maja Deković. (1990). The contribution of significant others to adolescents' self-esteem. *Adolescence, 25.100*, 839–846.

Laursen, Brett. (1993). The perceived impact of conflict on adolescent relationships. *Merrill-Palmer Quarterly, 39.4*, 535–550.

Levy, Susan R., Cydne Perhats, Myra Nash-Johnson, and Jean F. Welter. (1992). Reducing the risks in pregnant teens who are very young and those with mild mental retardation. *Mental Retardation, 50.4*, 195–205.

McGovern, Mary Ann. (1990). Sensitivity and reciprocity in the play of adolescent mothers and young fathers with their infants. *Family Relations, 39*, 427–431.

Miller, Brent C. (1993). Families, science, and values: Alternative views of parenting effects and adolescent pregnancy. *Journal of Marriage and the Family, 55*, 7–21.

Miller, Brent C., Josefina J. Card, Roberta L. Paikoff, and James L. Peterson (eds.). (1992). *Preventing adolescent pregnancy: Model programs and evaluation*. Newbury Park, CA: Sage.

Miller, S. (1981). *Children as parents: A progress report on a study of childbearing and childrearing among 12–15 year-olds*. Washington, DC: Child Welfare League of America.

Moore, K., M. Sims, and C. Betsey. (1986). *Choice and circumstances: Racial differences in adolescent sexuality and fertility*. New Brunswick, NJ: Transaction.

Musick, Judith S. (1993). *Young, poor, and pregnant: The psychology of teenage motherhood*. New Haven: Yale University Press.

Nathanson, M., B. Allen, and J. Jemall (1986). Family functioning and the adolescent mother: A systems approach. *Adolescence, 84.21*, 827–841.

Santoli, Al. (1995). When it's tougher here than over there. *Parade* (May 28), 4–6.

Sheehan, Susan. (1993). *Life for me ain't been no crystal stair*. New York: Pantheon.

Smith, P., and D. Munford (eds.). (1980). *Adolescent pregnancy: Perspective for health professionals*. Boston: Hall.

Voydanoff, Patricia, and Brenda W. Donnelly. (1990). *Adolescent sexuality and pregnancy*. Family Studies Text Series 12. Newbury Park, CA: Sage.

Whitman, T., J. Borkowski, C. Schellenbach, and P. Math. (1987). Predicting and understanding developmental delay of children of adolescent mothers: A multidimensional approach. *American Journal of Mental Deficiency, 92.1*, 46–50.

Zelnik, M., J. Kanter, and K. Ford. (1981). *Sex and pregnancy in adolescence.* Beverly Hills, CA: Sage.

Alternative Education

Bishop, G. (1989). *Alternative strategies for education.* New York: St. Martins.

Deal, Terrence E., and Robert R. Nolan (eds.). (1978). *Alternative schools: Ideologies, realities, guidelines.* Chicago: Nelson-Hall.

Eriksen, Aase, and Joseph Gantz. (1974). *Partnership in urban education: An alternative school.* Midland, MI: Pendell.

Takanishi, Ruby (ed.). (1993). *Adolescence in the 1990s.* Teachers College Record Series, edited by Ellen Condliffe Lagemann. New York: Teachers College.

Policy Issues

Bardach, E. (1984). *The implementation game: What happens after a bill becomes a law.* Cambridge, MA: MIT Press.

Bassett, B., and P. Johannes. (1983). Interorganizational communication. In R. Hall and R. Quinn (eds.), *Organizational theory and public policy,* 179–194. Beverly Hills, CA: Sage.

Campbell, A. (1968). The role of family planning in the reduction of poverty. *Journal of Marriage and the Family, 30.2,* 236–238.

Chase, G. (1979). Implementing a human services program: How hard will it be? *Public Policy, 27.4,* 387–435.

Dears, James T. (ed.). (1992). *Sexuality and the curriculum: The politics and practices of sexuality education.* New York: Teachers College.

Elmore, R. (1980). Organizational models of social program implementation. *Public Policy, 26.2,* 185–228.

Forrester, J. (1982). Planning in the face of power. *Journal of American Planning Association,* Winter, 67–80.

Guess, R. (1981). *The idea of a critical theory: Habermas and the Frankfurt school.* Cambridge: Cambridge University Press.

Hall, R., and R. Quinn (eds.). (1983). *Organizational theory and public policy.* Beverly Hills: Sage.

Jackson, Daney, and William Maddy. (1992). *Reference manual: Building coalitions.* The Ohio Center for Action on Coalition Development. Columbus: Ohio State University.

Kaufman, H.F. (1959). Toward an interactional conception of community. *Social Forces, 38,* 8–17.

Lachenmeyer, C. (1980). A complete evaluation design for community mental health programs. In M. Gibbs, J. Lachenmeyer, and J. Segal (eds.), *Community psychology: Theoretical and empirical approaches,* 339–361. New York: Gardner.

Lipsky, M. (1980). *Street level bureaucracy.* New York: Russell Sage Foundation.

Marshall, C., D. Mitchell, and F. Wirt. (1989). *Culture and education policy in the American states.* Hampshire, England: Falmer.

McGee, E. (1982). *Too little, too late: Services for teenage parents (working papers).* New York: Ford Foundation.

Millstein, Susan G., Anne C. Peterson, and Elena O. Nightingale (eds.). (1993). *Promoting the health of adolescents: New directions for the twenty-first century.* New York: Oxford University Press.

Moore, K. (1983). *School-age parents: Federal programs and policies relevant to pregnant and parenting secondary students.* Washington, DC: Urban Institute.

Mulford, C. (ed.). (1984). *Interorganizational relations: Implications for community development.* New York: Human Sciences Press.

Pittman, Karen J., and Michele Cahill. (1992). Youth and caring: The role of youth programs in the development of caring. Commissioned paper for Lilly Endowment.

Washington, DC: Center for Youth Development and Policy Research Academy of Educational Development.

Sears, James T. (ed.). (1992). *Sexuality and the curriculum: The politics and practices of sexuality education.* New York: Teachers College.

Sedlak, Michael W. (1983). Young women and the city: Adolescent deviance and the transformation of educational policy 1870–1960. *History of Education Quarterly, 23.1,* 1–28.

Sergiovanni, Thomas J. (1994). *Building community in schools.* San Francisco: Jossey-Bass.

Whyte, W.F. (1955). *Street corner society.* Chicago: Chicago University Press.

Research Methods

Cowen, E., and E. Gesten. (1980). Evaluating community programs: Tough and tender perspectives. In M. Gibbs, J. Lachenmeyer, and J. Segal (eds.), *Community psychology: Theoretical and empirical approaches,* 363–393. New York: Gardner.

Dokecki, P.R., and C.A. Heffinger. (1989). Strengthening families of young children with handicapping conditions: Mapping backward from street level. In J. Gallagher, P. Trohanis, and R.M. Clifford (eds.), *Policy implementation for children with special needs,* 59–84. Baltimore: Brooks.

Elmore, R. (1979–1980). Backward mapping: Implementation research and policy decisions. *Political Science Quarterly, 94.4,* 601–616.

Glaser, B., and A. Strauss. (1967). *The discovery of grounded theory: Strategies for qualitative research.* Chicago: Aldine.

Halpern, R. (1987). *Action research for the late 1980's.* Ann Arbor: University of Michigan Press.

Lincoln, Y., and E. Guba. (1985). *Naturalistic inquiry.* Beverly Hills, CA: Sage.

Marsh, Jeanne C. (1991). Services to teenage parents. *Evaluation and Program Planning, 14.1–2,* 1 (guest editor's introduction).

Marshall, C., and G. Rossman. (1989). *Designing qualitative research.* Newbury Park, CA: Sage.

McCall, G., and J.L. Simmons (eds.). (1969). *Issues in participant observation.* New York: Random House.

Rapoport, R. (ed.). (1985). *Children, youth, and families: The action-research relationship.* Cambridge, MA: Cambridge University Press.

Rossi, P., and H. Freeman. (1985). *Evaluation: A systematic approach* (3d ed.). Beverly Hills, CA: Sage.

Schatzman, L., and A. Strauss. (1973). *Field research: Strategies for natural sociology.* Englewood Cliffs, NJ: Prentice-Hall.

Spradley, J. (1979). *The ethographic interview.* New York: Holt.

Stainback, S., and W. Stainback (1988). *Understanding and conducting qualitative research.* Dubuque, IA: Kendall/Hunt.

Strauss, A.L. (1987). *Qualitative analysis for social scientists.* Cambridge: Cambridge University Press.

Yin, R.K. (1989). *Case study research: Design and methods.* Applied Social Research Methods Series 5. London: Sage.

Teenage Fathers

Barret, R., and B. Robinson. (1982a). A descriptive study of teenage expectant fathers. *Family Relations: Journal of Applied Family and Child Studies, 31.3,* 349–352.

———. (1982b). Teenage fathers: Neglected too long. *Social Work, 27.6,* 484–488.

Pannor, R., F. Massarik., and B. Evans. (1971). *Unmarried father: New approaches for helping unmarried young parents.* New York: Spring.

Sander, J.H., and J. Rosen. (1987). Teenage fathers working with the neglected partner in adolescent childbearing. *Family Planning Perspectives, 19.3,* 107–110.

Index